A Guide to
Divorce
in Missouri

Simple Answers
to Complex Questions

Cary J. Mogerman, Esq.
Joseph J. Kodner, Esq.

Addicus Books
Omaha, Nebraska

An Addicus Nonfiction Book

ISBN 978-1-940495-65-1

Typography Jack Kusler

This book is a general informational guide and it is not intended to serve as a substitute for an attorney. Nor is it the author's intent to give legal advice contrary to that of an attorney.

Library of Congress Cataloging-in-Publication Data
Names: Mogerman, Cary J., author. | Kodner, Joseph J., author.
Title: A guide to divorce in Missouri : simple answers to complex questions : a guide to the legal process, understanding your rights, and what to expect / Cary J. Mogerman, Esq.; Joseph J. Kodner, Esq.
Description: Omaha, Nebraska : Addicus Books, Inc., 2016. | Includes bibliographical references and index.
Identifiers: LCCN 2016012870 (print) | LCCN 2016013245 (ebook) | ISBN 9781940495651 (alk. paper) | ISBN 9781943886395 (PDF) | ISBN 9781943886401 (EPUB) | ISBN 9781943886418 (MOBI) Subjects: LCSH: Divorce—Law and legislation—Missouri—Miscellanea.
Classification: LCC KFM7900 .M64 2016 (print) | LCC KFM7900 (ebook) | DDC
346.77801/66--dc23
LC record available at http://lccn.loc.gov/2016012870

Addicus Books, Inc.
P.O. Box 45327
Omaha, Nebraska 68145
www.AddicusBooks.com
Printed in the United States of America
10 9 8 7 6 5 4 3 2 1

To my wife Dee, my family,
and all of my colleagues and staff here
at the firm, for all that they do every day.
CJM

To Holly, Emi and Miya, who provide me with
motivation and inspiration and to my co-workers at Zerman
Mogerman, LLC, who make working in a challenging field an
enjoyable experience.
JJK

Contents

Introduction

When it comes to the subject of divorce, the world does not suffer from a shortage of opinions. Family, friends, and acquaintances alike, freely share their perspectives, solicited or not, with you when they learn that you are going through the divorce process. Although undoubtedly well intentioned, the advice offered frequently fails to take into consideration the unique circumstances of your divorce.

The analogy of two high school students, taking the SAT exam in different years, presents a good example. Although each student goes through a similar process and faces similar challenges, the student who already took the exam telling the student who is scheduled to take the exam all of his answers to his exam provides no insight. Just as the questions and answers differ between different versions of the test, the issues and factors that impact the outcome of any two divorces are not the same. There are simply too many different variables to utilize any another result as a benchmark for your own. Most assuredly, you and your spouse do not have the same employment circumstances, lifestyle, or assets of those people whose divorce you think might provide an appropriate gauge for your own.

For many, the divorce process is a daunting one, full of uncertainty and confusion. By providing easy to understand answers to both basic and complex questions regarding divorce in Missouri, we hope to provide you with a foundation to help navigate through the divorce process.

Divorce touches nearly every aspect of your life and can result in many significant changes to your lifestyle. Throughout the process, you will face your fair share of difficult choices.

Undoubtedly, you will require a good deal of support throughout the journey. *A Guide to Divorce in Missouri* was written to provide practical information by answering many common questions for those going through a divorce. Hopefully these answers will provide some degree of support and help you navigate through this time of transition with more clarity and ease.

In no way shape or form is this book intended to be a substitute for advice from your lawyer. Rather, it is designed to assist you in working with your lawyer to reach your goals for the resolution of your divorce. The more you understand and appreciate about the process, the better you are able to make sound decisions regarding very challenging subjects. We hope you will use this book as a guide to ask your lawyer questions, to understand what it is you are unclear about, and to begin seeing the big picture of the course of action upon which you are about to embark.

1

Understanding the Divorce Process

Just the word "divorce," standing alone, can evoke an emotional, visceral response. Why? One reason is that at its root, divorce terminates what once represented a loving, mutually beneficial relationship. Although different people have different preconceived notions regarding divorce, frequently, these notions derive from sources that portray divorce in a less than realistic light. Without a frame of reference, the entire process can become overwhelming.

At a time when your life can feel like it's out of control, sometimes the smallest bit of predictability can bring a degree of comfort. The outcome of many aspects of your divorce and consequently your future will remain unknown while your divorce is pending. This lack of certainty may serve as a source of both fear and anxiety.

Most divorces proceed in a step-by-step manner. Despite the issues that are unique to your divorce, you can generally count on one phase of your divorce following the next. Sometimes just realizing you are completing stages and moving forward with your divorce can reassure you that it won't go on forever.

By developing an understanding of the divorce process, you can reduce the anxiety that comes along with being involved in an unfamiliar process. When your attorney starts talking about "depositions," "interrogatories" or "subpoenas," your understanding of the playing field, however basic, will give you the tools to cope. When you understand the function and value of each step in the divorce process, you will be prepared to deal with what comes next.

1

1.1 What is my first step in seeking a divorce?

Whether you have come to the conclusion to proceed with a divorce, your spouse has informed you of his/her intent to proceed with a divorce or you are merely exploring your options for what may later come to pass, taking the first step often proves difficult. Your divorce represents one of, if not the most, important legal and financial transactions of your life. As with any endeavor, how you start the process can significantly impact the final outcome. It therefore behooves you to take the right first steps, which, in most circumstances involves obtaining legal representation.

While anyone with a valid law license can represent you in a divorce proceeding, there are significant benefits to working with a law firm that handles divorces as a regular part of its law practice. Attorneys with experience in divorce have the knowledge and experience to guide you through the complexities and issues that they encounter on a daily basis.

With the proliferation of website optimization, attorney referral websites and ranking websites, the amount of information available may seem daunting. The attorney who advertises the most may not be the best choice. Oftentimes, the best recommendations come from people who have knowledge of a lawyer's experience and reputation. Regardless of the information you receive from others, it is critical that you select an attorney with whom you feel comfortable and whose approach to your case makes sense to you. You may have to meet with several lawyers before you find the right match.

Before your initial consultation ask what documents the lawyer would like you to bring with you. Make a list of your questions to bring to your first meeting. Start making plans for how you will pay your attorney to begin work on your case.

1.2 Must I have an attorney to get a divorce in Missouri?

No, but it is a good idea to do so. Proceeding without an attorney is not advised. Although not mandatory, hiring an attorney can aid you in innumerable ways. Foremost, an attorney will advise you of your rights and can inform you as to the range of likely outcomes in the event of trial. Very few spouses stand on equal ground with one another when it comes to bargaining power. More often than not, retaining an attorney helps to counteract this disparity and results in better-informed decision-making. Divorce judgments are products of legal proceedings, and carry with them numerous implications for the future including tax consequences, property rights, debt allocation, and indemnification rights. You will be far better served by investing in competent legal representation to insure that these issues are properly addressed than hoping for the best without an attorney.

If you are considering proceeding without an attorney, at a minimum have an initial consultation with an attorney to discuss your rights and duties under the law. Meeting with a lawyer can help you decide whether to proceed on your own. If you elect not to retain counsel, there are resources available through the courts to assist you in the divorce process. The Missouri judiciary at www.selfrepresent.mo.gov has established a webpage with information about self-representation. Call your local courthouse to see whether there is a self-help desk available to provide assistance.

1.3   What steps are taken during the divorce process?

While every person's divorce is unique, as a general matter, the typical divorce in Missouri involves the steps listed below.

- Obtain referrals for several attorneys.
- Schedule appointments for initial consultations with attorneys.
- Prepare a list of questions and gather relevant documents for your initial consultations.
- Meet for initial consultations with several different attorneys.
- Select the attorney that represents the best fit for your goals and approach.
- Carefully review the fee agreement and ask and resolve any questions you may have about its terms before you sign.
- Pay the attorney the agreed-upon fee or advance.
- Provide requested information and documents to your attorney, and take any other actions as advised by the attorney.

- The attorney will prepare the *petition for dissolution of marriage,* financial disclosures and, if applicable, motions for temporary orders for your review and signature.
- The attorney will prepare and file the petition for dissolution of marriage, and other required documents with clerk of the court.
- In consultation with your attorney, elect the method of how to serve your spouse with the petition for dissolution of marriage and associated paperwork. Service may be obtained via the sheriff, special process server or *voluntary entry of appearance* by your spouse or his or her attorney.
- After being served or entering their appearance, your spouse has thirty days within which to file responsive pleadings.
- If applicable, your attorney will address temporary (while the case remains pending) orders concerning issues including child custody and visitation, child support, spousal maintenance, access to the marital residence and attorney's fees and litigation expenses.
- If a mutually agreeable resolution regarding temporary issues cannot be reached, the court may hold a hearing and enter judgment on the temporary issues.
- If there are minor children, several, but not all Missouri counties require the parties to attend a parent education class.
- Both sides will conduct *discovery* to obtain information regarding relevant facts, and obtain valuations of assets. Appraisals may be necessary.
- Your attorney may advise you that it is necessary to retain experts to provide expert opinion testimony concerning various disputed issues.
- Confer with attorney to review facts, identify issues, assess strengths and weaknesses of your case, review strategy, and develop proposals for settlement.
- If the parties are able to reach agreement on all issues, one attorney will prepare the necessary settlement

documents for approval by the other side. There are frequently several revisions made back and forth.

OR

- The court will set a trial date. The procedure for setting trial differs between different counties and varies from obtaining a date near the outset of the case to obtaining a date only after all discovery has been completed.
- Pay trial retainer to fund the work needed to prepare for trial and services the day or days of trial.
- Parties prepare for trial on unresolved issues. This includes preparation of witnesses, trial exhibits, legal research on contested issues, pretrial motions, trial briefs, preparation of direct and cross-examination of witnesses, preparation of opening statement, subpoena of witnesses, closing argument and suggestions to the court.
- Meet with attorney for final trial preparation.
- Trial
- The trial judge may request proposed judgments from both sides.
- Judge prepares and signs decree of dissolution.
- The parties may file authorized posttrial motions including motions to amend the judgment, for new trial, and to reopen the evidence.
- After the judge rules on any posttrial motions, and the judgment has become final, the parties have the right to appeal the judgment.

1.4   Is Missouri a "no-fault" state or do I need grounds for a divorce?

Those filing for divorce frequently misunderstand the term "no fault" as it applies to divorce. Missouri law places it among the majority of states that have been given the label "no fault." This designation simply means that in order to obtain a divorce, neither you nor your spouse are required to prove that the other is "at fault" in order for the court to grant you a divorce. However, even though issues such as infidelity, abuse, and abandonment need not be proven to obtain a divorce, the party seeking the divorce must still prove that the marriage is "irretrievably broken."

This does not mean however, that issues of behavior do not play a role in the divorce process. Missouri law requires the court to consider the conduct of the parties during the marriage in both the division of marital property and the determination of spousal maintenance.

1.5   How will a judge view infidelity or my spouses' infidelity?

The trial court may take infidelity into account in your divorce. Although no Missouri statute refers specifically to infidelity, the statutes governing the division of marital property and spousal maintenance require the court to consider the conduct of the parties during the marriage. While infidelity certainly falls within the definition of conduct, it represents only one type of conduct out of many that the court may consider. The impact of infidelity on the division of property and spousal maintenance will vary according to several factors, including:

- When during the marriage the infidelity occurred
- The degree to which the extramarital relationship contributed to the irretrievable breakdown of the marriage
- The burden that the infidelity placed on the non-offending spouse
- The extent to which you or your spouse expended marital funds on the person with whom he/she was having an affair

The impact of infidelity may also vary. Trial judges possess a significant amount of discretion in weighing the factors that the Missouri statutes charge them with considering. Missouri statutes only require that judges consider certain factors. Nothing however, requires them to attach importance to any specific factor.

Unless a spouse's infidelity directly or indirectly impacts custody, the mere existence of an extramarital affair will not bear upon custody proceedings. However, the judge will consider evidence regarding inappropriate exposure of a child to an extramarital affair as well as evidence concerning a parent's dereliction of his or her parental obligations in favor of an extramarital relationship.

1.6 Do I have to get divorced in the same state in which my spouse and I were married?

No. Regardless of the state or country where you were married, you may seek a divorce in Missouri, so long as the jurisdictional requirements of residency are satisfied. Those requirements are addressed in the following question.

1.7 How long must I have lived in Missouri to get a divorce in the state?

Either you or your spouse must have been a resident of Missouri for at least ninety days immediately prior to the filing of the petition for dissolution of marriage to meet the residency requirement for a divorce in Missouri. Physical presence alone will not suffice for purposes of residency. In order to establish residency in Missouri for the purpose of obtaining a divorce, your physical presence in the state must be accompanied by an intention to remain indefinitely.

1.8 My spouse has told me she will never "give" me a divorce. Can I get one in Missouri anyway?

Yes, so long as you meet the residency requirements. In Missouri, spousal consent is not required to obtain a divorce. Your spouse may oppose the divorce by challenging your allegation that the marriage is irretrievably broken. If this occurs, you will bear the burden of proving the irretrievable breakdown to the court.

Should your spouse deny the irretrievable breakdown of the marriage, you may want to consider amending your petition to include a second count for legal separation. Legal separations share nearly all of the same characteristics of dissolutions of marriage, including the division of property and debt, custody determinations, child support awards and spousal maintenance awards. The only practical difference between the two is that in a legal separation you remain legally married. In Missouri, either party may unilaterally convert a legal separation to a dissolution of marriage after the elapse of ninety days following the entry of a legal separation.

1.9 Can I divorce my spouse in Missouri if he or she lives in another state?

Even if your spouse lives in another state, you can, at a minimum, obtain a divorce so long as you have met Missouri's residency requirements. Missouri recognizes the concept of a *divisible divorce*. A divisible divorce allows the courts to grant a divorce to anyone who has been a resident of the state for ninety days immediately preceding the filing of the petition for dissolution of marriage.

If your spouse does not meet the requirements for personal jurisdiction in Missouri, Missouri courts will not have the authority to determine the other issues that courts typically resolve in divorce proceedings, including spousal maintenance, child custody, child support and/or awards of property located out of the state. If Missouri lacks personal jurisdiction over your spouse, these issues will remain unresolved until a court that has jurisdiction over both you and your spouse can address them.

Because the determination of whether your spouse is subject to personal jurisdiction in Missouri depends on several factors, it is important that you inform your attorney about your spouse's connections to Missouri. Your attorney will discuss with you the facts that will need to be proven and the steps necessary to give your spouse proper notice to ensure that the court will have jurisdiction over your spouse.

1.10 Can I get a divorce even when I don't know where my spouse is currently living?

If you do not know the current whereabouts of your spouse, Missouri law allows you to proceed with a divorce by serving them through publication. In order to proceed in this manner, you will need to file a statement, under oath, listing your spouse's last known address and demonstrating why you cannot obtain service in the other manners authorized by Missouri law. Thereafter you must have a notice, which needs to include specific details of the litigation, published at least once a week for four consecutive weeks in a newspaper of general circulation in the county where you filed the petition for dissolution.

1.11 I just moved to a different county within the state of Missouri. Do I have to file in the county where my spouse lives?

You may file your petition for divorce in either the county where you reside or in the county where your spouse resides. Your spouse has the right to ask the court to transfer the proceeding to the county in which he or she resides. The court may grant this request if your children resided in the same county as your spouse during in the ninety days immediately before you filed the divorce proceeding, or if transferring the case would be in the best interest of your children because the children and at least one parent have a significant connection with the county, and substantial evidence concerning the present or future care, protection and personal relationships of the children exist in the county where your spouse resides.

1.12 I immigrated to Missouri. Will my immigration status stop me from getting a divorce?

If you meet the residency requirements for divorce in Missouri, you can get a divorce here. Talk to an immigration lawyer about the likelihood of a divorce leading to immigration challenges.

1.13 Is there a waiting period for a divorce in Missouri?

In Missouri you cannot get divorced until the petition for dissolution of marriage has been on file with the court for at least thirty days. Although not specified in the statute, many judges will not grant a divorce until thirty days after the court determines that the *respondent,* the person who did not initiate the divorce process, was given proper legal notice of the divorce. This date is either the day that the respondent is personally served with papers or the date that the respondent or an attorney on his or her behalf files with the court either a waiver of service or "entry of appearance" with the court.

1.14   What is a *divorce petition*?

A *divorce petition,* also referred to as a *petition for dissolution of marriage,* is a document signed by the person filing for divorce and filed with the court to initiate the divorce process. The petition needs to contain certain information required by Missouri statutes, including the basis for the court's jurisdiction. The petition must also provide the specific relief, such as spousal maintenance, custody awards and child support, that the plaintiff is asking the court to ultimately order. A sample divorce petition is available in the Appendix.

1.15   My spouse said she filed for divorce last week, but my lawyer says there's nothing on file at the courthouse. What does it mean to "file for divorce?"

A filing for divorce involves the submission of all of the necessary documents in the appropriate court to initiate legal proceedings. Until the court has accepted those documents, the case has not yet been filed. There are many reasons why the court might reject an initial filing, including failure to file required documents, or failure to pay the filing fee.

If your spouse has received permission from the court to file the case under seal or under initials, your attorney might not have sufficient information to locate the filing either at the courthouse or online. Although many counties in Missouri have adopted e-filing, as of the date of the publication of this book, not all counties have adopted the system.

1.16   If we both want a divorce, does it matter who files?

From a purely legal perspective, the *petitioner* (the party who files the complaint initiating the divorce process) and the *respondent* (the other spouse) are not viewed differently by the court based upon which party filed. The court, as a neutral decision maker, will not give preference to either party, and both parties will be given equal consideration; each will have a chance to be heard and present arguments.

1.17   Are there advantages to filing first?

Some attorneys believe that at trial there may be a tactical advantage to presenting your side of the case first. Others disagree. If you have the luxury of having the opportunity to decide whether to file first, you should discuss the pros and cons with your attorney. Each case presents different issues and with it, different potential benefits and/or detriments associated with filing first.

1.18 Can I stop the newspaper from publishing notice of the filing or granting of my divorce?

Documents filed with the court, such as a divorce petition or a final decree are matters of public record. Newspapers have a right to access this information, and many newspapers publish this information as a matter of routine.

In rare cases, a divorce file may be kept private, referred to as being "sealed" or "under seal" if the court so orders. The court also has the ability to allow only the parties' initials to be used as opposed the parties' full names. Again, this is requires judicial approval, which is typically only given under special circumstances.

1.19 Is there a way to avoid embarrassing my spouse and not have the sheriff serve him with the divorce papers at his workplace?

There are several ways to simultaneously ensure that your spouse becomes a party to the litigation and avoid the potentially embarrassing situations associated with service. One option involves using a special process server to serve your spouse instead of the sheriff. Although this costs more than using the sheriff, you have significantly more control over the process. Once the court approves a special process server, you can instruct the special process server not to serve your spouse at his or her workplace.

Similarly, if you do not believe that your spouse will attempt to avoid service, you can ask the special process server to coordinate with your spouse a mutually agreeable time and place to effectuate service. Additionally, if the circumstances warrant, you can give your spouse the opportunity to sign a document known as a *waiver of service and voluntary appearance.* Talk to your lawyer about what options for having your spouse served make the most sense given the circumstances of your particular case.

Divorce in Missouri

The use of a voluntary appearance is not appropriate for all cases, so discuss with your attorney the best choice for your case.

1.20 Should I sign a waiver of service and voluntary entry appearance even if I don't agree with what my spouse has written in the complaint for divorce?

If you have retained an attorney, he or she can file an entry of appearance on your behalf. This will not only avoid the need for service by the sheriff or special process server, but also will place both the opposing party and court on notice that counsel represents you.

If you have elected to forego representation, under ordinary circumstances signing a waiver of service and voluntary appearance simply eliminates the need for service of the petition and related court documents; it does not mean that you agree with anything your spouse has alleged in his or her petition for dissolution. However, you should, as with every document you sign, carefully review language of the proposed entry to make sure that you are not waiving other rights. A sample waiver of service and voluntary entry appearance is available in the Appendix.

1.21 Why should I contact an attorney right away if I have received divorce papers?

There are numerous reasons to seek legal representation as early as possible after having been served. Foremost amongst those reasons is the fact that petitions are time-sensitive documents. You have limited time after having been served within which to file responsive pleadings. Failure to file responsive pleadings in a timely manner may result in the court entering default judgment against you—a judgment which provides the other party with all of the relief sought by that party, without further notice or input to you. The effects of a default judgment may be devastating to the defaulting party.

While there are procedural means that allow you to attempt to set aside a default judgment, they may not be appropriate to all circumstances, and the safest practice is to avoid a default by responding within the time allowed.

12

1.22   What is an *ex parte court order?*

A party obtains an *ex parte court order* by going before the judge to request relief without giving prior notice or an opportunity to be heard to the other side. *Ex parte* orders are generally limited to emergency situations and are temporary in nature. Because of the potential for damage arising from an *ex parte* order, the judge will require the person requesting an *ex parte* order to post a bond.

If the judge grants an *ex parte* order, the order will remain in effect until a full hearing on the issue can be held. With the exception of adult abuse orders of protection and child orders of protection, judges are reluctant to sign *ex parte* orders. As a general matter, courts prefer that the other side be provided with notice of any requests for court orders, and have an opportunity to be heard before entering any orders.

1.23   What is a *motion?*

A *motion* is a written or oral request made to the court by a party to a lawsuit that seeks that the entry of a court order of some type. There are countless different types of motions that may be filed throughout the course of any one case. Some motions are designed to address procedural matters and others are designed to address substantive matters. While the vast majority of motions are written, in certain circumstances, a motion may be made orally. Oral motions arise when an issue arises while the parties are already before the court during a hearing or trial.

There are two basic types of motions, *testimonial motions* and *non-testimonial motions.* Non-testimonial motions generally do not involve any disputed facts. The attorneys appear before the judge and orally argue the merits of the motion. This may be done off the record in the judge's chambers or in open court either on or off the record. Testimonial motions, as their name indicates, require testimony on the record. These motions frequently involve disputed facts that necessitate the presentation of evidence by each side. When the judge rules on a motion, he or she will sign an order that makes a determination on the issue.

1.24 After my petition for divorce is filed, how soon can a temporary hearing be held to decide what happens with our child and our finances while the divorce is pending?

As a general rule, after your spouse has been served, the court can hear a motion for temporary orders upon proper notice to the other side. However, practically speaking, many courts will not entertain a non-emergency temporary orders motion until after an attorney has entered his or her appearance or until after an answer to the petition has been filed. Some judicial circuits have more specific rules about the scheduling of motions for temporary orders.

1.25 How much notice will I get if my spouse seeks a temporary order?

The statute that authorizes temporary orders allows the responding party ten days within which to file an answer. Unless a judge agrees to shorten time, Missouri law requires that a party be served no later than five days before the time specified for hearing.

1.26 During my divorce, what am I responsible for doing?

Some judicial circuits impose mandatory orders and place restrictions on litigants involved in a dissolution of marriage. However, even if your divorce is not pending in one of these circuits, there are several things that you should do that can make the divorce process easier for you and your attorney.

Those things include:

- Staying in regular contact with your attorney. Divorce cases are fluid and facts important to your cases are constantly evolving. Therefore, it is critical that you keep your attorney apprised of new developments in a timely manner.

- Updating your attorney regarding any changes in your contact information, such as address, phone numbers, and e-mail address

- Providing your attorney with all requested documents in a timely matter. Do not filter the documents you provide your attorney based upon your own determinations of relevance. Provide all requested documents to your attorney and let him or her decide which ones are important.

- Appearing in court on time
- Being direct about asking any questions you might have
- Telling your attorney your thoughts on settlement or what you would like the judge to order in your case
- Remaining respectful toward your spouse throughout the process
- Keeping your children out of the litigation
- Complying with any temporary court orders, such as restraining or support orders

1.27 I'm worried that I won't remember to ask my lawyer about all of the issues in my case. How can I be sure I don't miss anything?

Write down all of the topics you want to discuss with your attorney as they come to you, so that you do not forget any of the issues the next time you speak with your attorney. It is also important to maintain a dialogue with your attorney regarding your goals and expectations for the outcome of the divorce. Your lawyer's experience will be helpful in shaping and adjusting your reasonable expectations based upon what happens throughout your case. The checklist on the following pages provides a multitude of common issues to use as a starting point in your conversation with your attorney.

Divorce Issues Checklist

Issue	Notes
Dissolution of the marriage	
Custody of minor children	
Legal custody	
Physical custody / Visitation schedule	
Parenting Plan	
Relocation of children from jurisdiction	
Child support	
Deviation from child-support guidelines	
Work-related child care expenses	
Health insurance on minor children (including dental and vision)	
Uninsured / unreimbursed medical expenses for minor children	
Qualified medical support order	
Private school tuition for children	
College expenses for children	
Dependency exemptions	
Abatement of child support	
Travel expenses to facilitate parenting time for out-of-town/state parents	
Spousal maintenance	
Life insurance as security for maintenance	
Automatic wage withholding for support	
Temporary orders	
Health insurance	
Division of property	
Real property: marital residence	
Real property: rentals, vacation homes, commercial property, time shares, etc.	

Divorce Issues Checklist (Continued)

Issue	Notes
Retirement accounts and pensions	
Federal or military pensions	
Business interests	
Bank accounts	
Investment/securities accounts	
Stock options/grants	
Stock purchase plans	
Life insurance policies	
Frequent flyer miles	
Credit card points	
Separate/non-marital assets	
Separate/non-marital debts	
Pets	
Personal property division: including motor vehicles, recreation vehicles, campers, airplanes, collections, furniture, electronics, tools, household goods, etc.	
Division of marital debt	
Filing status for tax returns for last/current year	
Former name restoration	
Attorney fees	

1.28   My spouse has all of our financial information. How will I be able to prepare for negotiations and trial if I don't know the facts or have the documents?

You should not be asked to negotiate without the information you require to make an informed decision. After your divorce has been filed with the court, your attorney will proceed with a process known as *discovery*. Through the discovery process, which is described in greater detail in chapter 5, your attorney can ask your spouse as well as third parties to provide the documents and information need to prepare your case.

1.29 My spouse and I both want our divorce to be amicable. How can we keep it that way?

It is commendable that you and your spouse desire to remain amicable with one another as you move through the divorce process. Even under the best of circumstances, the divorce process can be challenging. Your interests will be at odds with your spouse over a great many issues. Not only are you bringing about an end to your status as a married couple, you are determining custodial arrangements for the children, separating your finances, and determining support. While remaining amicable will not always be easy, doing so will not only make the divorce process easier it will likely save you money on attorney fees.

Throughout your divorce, the attorney you select to represent you will be the face of your positions to both the court and your spouse's attorney. This fact makes your choice of an attorney very important. You should select an attorney who understands your goals and with whom you can agree on an approach to your case.

In order to keep things amicable, you may wish to discuss the options of mediation and negotiation with your attorney. Even if you are not able to settle all of the issues in your divorce, these actions can increase the likelihood of agreement on many of the terms of your divorce decree.

1.30 Can I pick my judge?

No. Neither the parties nor the attorneys have the ability to choose the judge who will be hearing the case. Under Missouri law, so long as the motion is filed in a timely manner, each side has the right to one automatic change of judge. Once your automatic change of judge has been used,you still have the ability to request a change of judge "for cause." A motion for change of judge for cause may be warranted if you believe that your judge has a *conflict of interest* that impacts his or her ability to render an impartial decision. Examples of conflicts of interest include, pre-existing relationships, shared financial interests, and prejudgment of the case. However, there are many factors, which you should discuss with your attorney before making the decision to file a motion for change of judge.

1.31   How long will it take to get my divorce?

The answer to this question varies case to case. The divorce of a client who comes in the door and tells you that he and his wife have already agreed upon a mutually acceptable resolution to all issues is likely to take much less time than a client who comes in ready to wage World War III. At the very minimum, there will be a thirty-day wait from the date of the filing of the divorce petition.

The more complex the issues involved in your case, the longer the case is likely to take. A few examples of complex issues include business valuations, contested custody disputes, and cases involving multiple real estate holdings.

1.32   What is the significance of my divorce being final?

The finality of your divorce decree, sometimes referred to as the decree of dissolution of marriage, is important for many reasons. It affects your right to remarry, your eligibility for health insurance from your former spouse, and your filing status for income taxes.

1.33   When does my divorce become final?

Your divorce becomes final for different purposes on different dates. The date that triggers the time period for a divorce becoming final is the date that the divorce decree is entered by court.

For most purposes, your divorce is final forty days from the date it is entered by the court. The trial judge retains control over the judgment for a period of thirty days after it has been entered. The judgment becomes final for purposes of appeal ten days after the thirty days has elapsed.

However, if either party files an authorized posttrial motion the thirty-day period that the trial judge retains control over the judgment expands to ninety days. The judgment then becomes final for purposes of appeal ten days after the court rules on the authorized posttrial motion or, if the court does not rule on the posttrial motion, ten days after the expiration of the ninety-day period.

19

For the purposes of collection on the judgment, your divorce is final upon its entry. While you have the right to commence collection efforts immediately upon the entry of the judgment, you may be forced to return the funds you obtain via execution or garnishment if the trial judge subsequently amends the judgment or the court of appeals reverses the trial court. The spouse against whom collection is sought may stop collection on the judgment by posting a bond set by the trial court.

1.34 Can I start using my former name right away and how do I get my name legally restored?

Once the court grants your name change, you may begin using your new name immediately. As a practical matter, you may find that certain agencies and institutions will not alter their records without a copy of court order that granted the name change.

If you want your former name restored, let your attorney know so that this provision can be included in both the petition for dissolution and the divorce decree. You still have the ability to change your legal name after your divorce has concluded, however, you will have to initiate a separate legal action for a name change.

2

Coping with Stress during the Divorce Process

Divorce adds an additional layer of stress to the normal, everyday stressors in your life. Although your relationship with your spouse was likely strained prior to the divorce filing, once you are engrossed in a divorce, the partnership you once relied upon no longer exists as a source of support. It may have been a few years ago. Or, it may have been many years ago. Perhaps it was only months. But, when you said, "I do," you meant it. Like most people getting married, you planned to be a happily married couple for life.

But things happen. Life brings change. People change. Whatever the circumstance, you now find yourself considering divorce. The emotions of divorce run from one extreme to another as you journey through the process. You may feel relief and ready to move on with your life. On the other hand, you may feel emotions that are quite painful. Anger. Fear. Sorrow. A deep sense of loss or failure. Remember, it is important to find support for coping with all these strong emotions.

Because going through a divorce can be an emotional time, having a clear understanding of the divorce process and what to expect will help you make better decisions. And, when it comes to decision-making, search inside yourself to clarify your intentions and goals for the future. Let these intentions be your guide.

2.1   My spouse left home weeks ago. I don't want a divorce because I feel our marriage can be saved. Should I still see an attorney?

Meeting with an attorney is not acknowledgement by you that your marriage is irretrievably broken, nor does not mean that a divorce will in fact occur. Because divorce lawyers deal with divorce every day, they may have some helpful advice on how to preserve your marriage. A good divorce lawyer wants what is best for the client. Not infrequently, reconciliation, counseling or some path other than divorce represents the best course of action.

It never hurts to see an attorney to discuss your current situation and find out what options you have at your disposal. Whether you want a divorce or not, there may be important actions for you to take now to protect your assets, credit, home, children, and future right to support.

2.2   The thought of going to a lawyer's office to talk about divorce is more than I can bear. I canceled the first appointment I made because I just couldn't do it. What should I do?

Many people have this type of reaction. While meeting with an attorney may add anxiety and stress to the other emotions you are dealing with, it is no different than going to see your doctor to deal with an illness. In both circumstances, a trip to the professional will not only help you understand your circumstances, but also create a plan of action to deal with whatever challenge you may be facing.

If you do not think that you can manage a first appointment without the moral support of a close relative or friend, you should ask the attorney if he or she is willing to allow this third party to participate in your meeting. You should know, however, that any of your communications with the attorney that include the presence of unnecessary third parties will not be protected by the attorney-client privilege. As such, the content of the communications may be discoverable by your spouse. However, if the presence of a relative or close friend will facilitate the meeting, most attorneys will not object.

2.3   There is some information about my marriage that I think my attorney needs, but I'm too embarrassed to discuss it. Must I tell the attorney?

Yes. Keeping critical information about your case secret from your attorney will impair his or her ability to represent you. The information you provide to an attorney helps them not only understand your story, but also guides them in the strategy they formulate to pursue your case. If you leave out important pieces of information due to embarrassment, you impair your attorney's ability to assess the merits of your case. Although you may be embarrassed, you should know that your attorney has an ethical duty to maintain confidentiality.

Unless you authorize your attorney to disclose the information, your lawyer is obligated to keep it private. Family law attorneys have heard it all. They are accustomed to hearing a lot of sensitive information from clients about both themselves and their families. While it may be deeply personal to you, it is unlikely that anything you tell your lawyer will come as a shock.

2.4   I'm unsure about how to tell our children about the divorce, and I'm worried I'll say the wrong thing. What's the best way?

How you and your spouse inform your children about the divorce as well as your later communications with them concerning the divorce will depend upon their ages and levels of maturity. There is no easy way or approved script to convey to your children the fact that you and your spouse will be divorcing. Simpler answers are best for young children. Avoid giving them more information than they need. After the initial discussion, keep the door open to further talks by creating opportunities for them to talk about the divorce. Use these times to acknowledge their feelings and offer support. Always assure them that the divorce is not their fault and that they are still loved by both you and your spouse, regardless of the divorce.

Do not share information about legal proceedings, meetings with lawyers or issues you are having with your spouse with your children. Use the adults in your life as a source of support to meet your own emotional needs.

Changes in your children's everyday lives, such as a change of residence or one parent leaving the home, are frequently one of the most important aspects of divorce to them. Maintaining continuity for your children, especially with respect to their regular patterns, will help them to better cope with the transitions that accompany a divorce.

2.5   My youngest child seems very depressed about the divorce, the middle one is angry, and my teenager is skipping school. How can I cope?

All children react to divorce differently. Some may push for a reconciliation, while others may act out at home or school. Reducing the level of conflict with your spouse, remaining a consistent and nurturing parent, and making sure both parents remain involved are all actions that can support your children regardless of how they are reacting to the divorce.

If your children are struggling with the divorce or you notice concerning changes in their behavior you should not hesitate to seek out outside help. Support groups for children whose parents are divorcing are also available at many schools and religious communities. School counselors can also provide some support. If more help is needed, confer with a therapist experienced in working with children.

2.6   I am so frustrated by my spouse's "Disneyland parent" behavior. Is there anything I can do to stop this?

After you and your spouse are no longer residing under the same roof, your family's everyday routines change. Frequently, feelings of guilt, competition, or remorse accompany these changes and can lead a parent to be tempted to spend his or her parenting time differently than they have historically. A typically uninvolved parent may suddenly insist on attending doctor visits, participating in after school activities or driving carpool. Other parents may choose to over indulge the children with trips to the toy store and frequent special activities. Additionally, a parent may, in an effort to become the favored parent or to make the time "special," elect to discipline the children in a more lenient manner.

Because there is little you can do to control how your spouse parents the children during his or her parenting time, you may try shifting your focus to your own behavior, and doing your utmost to be the best parent you can be to your children during this time. This includes keeping regular routines for your children for family meals, bedtimes, chores, and homework. Encourage family activities, as well as individual time with each child, when it's possible. During the time when a child's life is changing, providing a consistent and stable routine in your home can ease his or her anxiety and provide comfort.

2.7   Between requests for information from my spouse's lawyer and my own lawyer, I am totally overwhelmed. How do I manage gathering all of this detailed information by the deadlines imposed?

First, take a deep breath. Ask your attorney to help you prioritize all of the things you need to do. Although the demands of litigation can be strenuous, it helps to know what items require immediate attention and which ones may be put on the back burner.

Many of things you will be asked to do have deadlines. For that reason, it is important to start work on your tasks early. By starting immediately, you can avoid the unnecessary stress that comes along with coming up against the deadline. Break down your assignments into smaller, more manageable tasks.

If you are not a naturally organized person, ask for assistance from the support staff at your attorney's office. A paralegal may be able to make your job easier by giving you suggestions or help. If you genuinely do not believe that you will be able to complete the tasks that have been asked of you, communicate this to your attorney at your earliest opportunity. He or she may be able to coordinate an extension with your spouse's attorney, or, failing that, file a motion to extend the deadline.

2.8   I am so depressed about my divorce that I'm having difficulty getting out of bed in the morning to care for my children. What should I do?

Seek out help from a qualified health care provider. Your lawyer is not a mental health professional and although he or she will likely be sympathetic to your difficulties, he or she will not be equipped to offer you competent guidance in this area.

Although feelings of sadness are common during a divorce, more serious depression requires professional support. Even if you are not depressed, you may want to consider seeking guidance from a qualified therapist throughout the divorce process to help you cope with the challenges

Your health and your ability to care for your children are both essential. Follow through on recommendations by your health care professionals for therapy, medication, or other measures to improve your wellness.

2.9   Will taking prescribed medication to help treat my insomnia and depression hurt my case?

Unless you abuse your medications or take prescription medications not prescribed to you by your physician, the fact that you are on medication should not negatively impact your case. Although the condition for which you take medication may brought up in the context of custody determination, it is far better to be proactive in dealing with the condition than ignoring it or not following doctor's orders.

Taking care of your health is of the utmost importance during this difficult time, and will serve your best interest as well as the best interest of your children. Do not neglect to inform your attorney of any medications that you are taking, treatments that you are receiving, or any changes to your health status or prescribed medications.

2.10   I know I need help to cope with the stress of the divorce, but I can't afford counseling. What can I do?

If you need support, but cannot afford to hire your own counselor or therapist, there are a number of alternatives you may want to consider, including:

- Meeting with a member of the clergy or lay chaplain
- Joining a divorce support group
- Contacting a social agency that offers counseling services on a sliding-fee scale
- Turning to friends and family members

Additionally, there are several resources included at the back of this book that should be consulted to help determine if free counseling is available to you. If none of these options are available, look again at your budget. You may see that counseling is important enough that you decide to find a way to increase your income or lower your expenses to support this investment in your well-being.

2.11   I'm the one who filed for divorce, but I still have loving feelings toward my spouse and feel sad about divorcing. Does this mean I should dismiss my divorce?

Ongoing feelings toward your spouse often persist long after a divorce is filed. The filing of the divorce action does not flip a switch that turns off all of your feelings for your spouse. Whether or not to proceed with a divorce is a deeply personal decision. However, before you make any decisions on emotion alone, you should try to take a step back and consider all of the relevant factors, including those that led you to file for divorce.

Ask yourself whether you believe that you and your spouse have a realistic chance at reconciliation. Has your spouse demonstrated a willingness to be proactive and address the issues that brought the two of you to the cusp of divorce?

The answer to this question can help you decide whether to consider reconciliation. Talk to your therapist, coach, or spiritual advisor to help determine the right path for you.

2.12   Will my lawyer charge me for the time I spend talking about my feelings about my spouse and my divorce?

Yes. Unless you have a flat-fee arrangement with your attorney, you should expect to pay your attorney for his or her time, regardless of the topic of discussion. Remember that although your attorney may be a sympathetic ear, the money you expend paying him or her to discuss your feelings may be better spent on a counselor or therapist.

2.13   My lawyer doesn't seem to realize how difficult my divorce is for me. How can I get him to understand?

Everyone wants support and compassion from the professionals who help during a divorce. Speak frankly with your attorney about your concerns. It may be that your lawyer does not see your concerns as being relevant to the job of getting your desired outcome in the divorce. Your willingness to improve the communication will help your lawyer understand how best to support you in the process and will help you understand which matters are best left for discussion with your therapist or a supportive friend.

2.14 I've been told not to speak ill of my spouse in front of my child, but I know she's doing this all the time. Why can't I just speak the truth?

Regardless of what you suspect your spouse may or may not be saying to your children, it is critically important to avoid bad-mouthing your spouse in their presence. Even though you are divorcing your spouse, your children are not. It can be devastating for them to hear you make negative comments about the other parent. Your children need to have a safe environment in which it is permissible to love and respect both parents, without fear of repercussions. The best way to support your child during this time is to encourage a positive relationship with the other parent.

Let your attorney know if you learn that your spouse is speaking negatively about you to your children or discussing inappropriate topics. He or she can address the issue with the other attorney or seek relief from the court, if necessary.

2.15 Nobody in our family has ever been divorced and I feel really ashamed. Will my children feel the same way?

The divorce will bring many inevitable changes in your life and the lives of your children. Although your children may be disappointed, sad, or upset that their parents are divorcing, shame need not be an emotion they need to feel as a result of the divorce. You can help foster a sense of pride in the new family dynamic and encourage them to look forward to the future with confidence and a sense of security.

Your children will have an opportunity to witness you overcoming obstacles, demonstrating independence, and moving forward in your life notwithstanding challenges. You can be a great teacher to them during this time by demonstrating pride in your family and in yourself.

2.16 I am terrified of having my deposition taken. My spouse's lawyer is very aggressive, and I'm afraid I'm going to say something that will hurt my case.

A deposition is an opportunity for your spouse's attorney to ask you questions face to face, while you are under oath. Attorneys use this particular discovery tool to gather information, to pin you down to certain answers or opinions, and to evaluate the type of witness you will be if the case proceeds to trial. Feelings of anxiety and concern about your deposition are perfectly normal.

Regardless of the personality of the lawyers involved, most depositions in divorces are quite uneventful. Remember that your attorney will be seated by your side at all times to support you and object to improper questions. If the other attorney becomes abusive, your attorney has the right to stop the deposition to seek a protective order from the court.

Meet with your lawyer in advance to prepare for your deposition. If you are worried about certain questions that might be asked, talk to your attorney about them. Have your attorney ask you some practice questions to get a sense of what to expect.

2.17 I am still so angry with my spouse; how can I be expected to sit in the same room during a settlement conference?

Sitting in the same room with your soon-to-be ex-spouse may be very challenging. However, you must remember that you are in court and conduct yourself with the proper level of decorum. If you quarrel with your spouse or cause a scene in the courtroom, you are very likely impacting the judge's opinion of you.

If the anger you have toward your spouse is so great that you cannot stand to be in same room, ask your attorney to arrange to have you sit in a place outside of the courtroom where he or she can find you if needed. That way you can still participate if called upon to do so. You might also consider seeking counseling to support you with coping with your feelings of anger.

2.18 I'm afraid I can't make it through court without having an emotional breakdown. How do I prepare?

Appearing in court for non-divorce related reasons could cause apprehension and fear. When you come to court for a divorce, for some, the experience may prove even more challenging. A divorce trial can be an emotionally charged time, requiring lots of support. Some of these ideas may help you through the process:

- Meet with your lawyer or the firm's support staff in advance of your court date to prepare you for your testimony as well as what to expect in court.

- Ask your lawyer whether there are any documents you should review in preparation for trial, such as your deposition, interrogatory responses, and trial exhibits.

- Visit the courtroom in advance to familiarize yourself with the surroundings.

- Ask your lawyer about having a support person (one who will not also be a witness in your case) accompany you to court your trial date.

- Ask yourself what is the worst thing that could happen and consider what options you would have if it did.

- Avoid alcohol, eat healthfully, exercise, and have plenty of rest during the period of time leading up to the court date. Each of these will help you to prepare for the stresses of the day.

- Plan what you intend to wear in advance. Small preparations may help to lower your stress.

- Visualize the experience going well. Picture yourself sitting in the witness chair, giving clear, confident, and truthful answers to easy questions.

- Allow yourself plenty of time by arriving early. Whether you are going to the court first or to your attorney's office first, make sure you have a plan for parking your car and arriving on time. Make sure to leave extra time in the event you encounter unexpected traffic.

- Take slow, deep breaths. Breathing deeply will steady your voice, calm your nerves, and improve your focus.

Your attorney will be prepared to support you throughout the proceedings. By taking the above steps, you can increase the ease of your experience.

2.19 I am really confused. One day I think the divorce is a mistake; the next day I know I can't go back, and a few minutes later I can hardly wait to be single again. Some days I just don't believe I'm getting divorced. What's happening?

Denial, transition, and acceptance are common passages for a person going through a divorce. One moment you might feel excited about your future and a few hours later you think your life is ruined.

It may be helpful to remember is that you may not pass from one stage to the next in a direct line. Feelings of anger or sadness may well up in you long after you thought you had moved on. Similarly, your mood might feel bright one day as you think about your future plans, even though you still miss your spouse.

Taking good care of yourself is essential during this period of your life. What you are going through requires a tremendous amount of energy. Allow yourself to experience your emotions, but also continue moving forward with your life. These steps will help your life get easier day-by-day.

3

Working with Your Attorney

A divorce is not a legal matter that you simply turn over to an attorney to handle on your behalf. To the contrary, a divorce requires frequent and meaningful collaboration between both attorney and client throughout. Your active involvement in the case will play an important role. Look at your relationship with your attorney as a partnership, the goal of which is to achieve a positive outcome that will set you up to carry on with your life after the divorce.

The counsel of your attorney can affect your life for years to come. So, the attorney you select to represent you should be a trusted and supportive advocate. Investing the time and energy to locate an attorney with whom you can engage in open and honest communications will return positive dividends.

3.1 Where do I begin looking for an attorney for my divorce?

If you have never had any experience in the legal system, this may be the first time you have needed to hire an attorney. For the most part, family law attorneys do little repeat business and rely on word of mouth and reputation for new clientele. Accordingly, you might consider asking friends and family members who have gone through a divorce, for their recommendations. If they thought they had a good lawyer, they may recommend him or her. They might also recommend their former spouse's lawyer. If you know anyone in the legal profession, ask for a referral to an attorney who is experienced in family law.

You may also consider consulting your local bar association to find out whether they have a referral service. Be sure to specify that you are looking for an attorney who handles divorce. The American Bar Association and the Missouri Bar Association have divisions or "sections" devoted to the practice of family law. Many members of these sections of law practice within the bar can be considered to be experienced in the practice of family law. Also, the American Academy of Matrimonial Lawyers, an organization limited to experienced family law attorneys who have been subjected to peer-review evaluation and who have passed state and national examinations on family law, maintains a list of its members online at www.aaml.org.

Many attorneys have websites that provide information on their practices areas, professional associations, experience, and philosophy. In recent years numerous attorney rating and referral sites have cropped up. You should always view these with a critical eye, because many of them are nothing more than paid advertisements.

3.2   How do I choose the right attorney?

Choosing the right attorney for your divorce is an important decision that will affect the trajectory of your entire divorce. Your attorney should be a trusted professional with whom you feel comfortable sharing information openly. He or she should be a person you can trust and a zealous advocate for your interests.

You will rely upon your attorney to help you make many decisions throughout the course of your divorce. You will also entrust your legal counsel to make a range of strategic and procedural decisions on your behalf. Feel free to seek all of the information you need to help you feel secure in knowing you have made the right choice.

Find an attorney who practices primarily in the family law area. Although many attorneys handle divorces, it is likely you will have more effective representation from an attorney who already knows the fundamentals of divorce law in Missouri.

Determine the level of experience you want in your attorney. For example, if you have had a short marriage, and few assets, an attorney with lesser experience might be a good value for your legal needs. However, if you are anticipating a custody dispute or have complex or substantial assets, a more experienced attorney may better meet your needs.

Consider the qualities in an attorney that are important to you. Even the most experienced and skilled attorney is not right for every person. Ask yourself what you are really looking for in an attorney so you can make your choice with these standards in mind.

It is important that you be confident in the attorney you hire. If you're unsure about whether the lawyer is really listening to you or understanding your concerns, keep looking until you find one who will. Your divorce is an important matter. It's critical that you have a professional you can trust.

3.3   Should I hire a "bulldog"—a very aggressive attorney?

The attorney you hire to represent you in your divorce should possess several qualities you are looking for. Although aggressiveness may be one of the traits you consider important, it would likely be a mistake to make your choice of an attorney based on aggressiveness alone. Take the time to make a list of the qualities in an attorney that are important to you. This "bulldog" may promise a "scorched earth" approach to the divorce which may do significant damage to your children, your relationship with your spouse, and your financial well-being. This could also have other adverse repercussions both during and after the divorce.

Additionally, expect the cost of your divorce to markedly increase if your attorney is unwilling to negotiate and drags your spouse into court at every opportunity. Look for a lawyer who can represent you with zealous advocacy, while at the same time maintains a high level of courtesy, professionalism, and integrity. Qualities which are likely far more advantageous than being aggressive include: preparation, diligence, candor, knowledge of the law, accessibility to the client, experience in both trial practice and negotiation, a respected reputation, and a capacity to defuse adversarial situations.

3.4   Should I interview more than one attorney?

It is the best policy to interview more than one attorney. Every lawyer has different strengths and styles; it is important that you choose the one that is right for you. Sometimes it is only by meeting with more than one attorney that you see clearly who will best be able to help you reach your goals in the way you want. Changing lawyers in the middle of litigation can be stressful and costly. It is wise to invest energy at the outset in making the right choice.

3.5   My spouse says because we're still friends we should use the same attorney for the divorce. Is this a good idea?

No. Plain and simple. It is ethically impermissible for one attorney to represent both spouses in an action for divorce. Even the most amicable of divorcing couples have differing interests. Although spouses may retain an attorney to mediate their divorce or draft settlement documents, that attorney cannot "represent" both parties at the same time. An attorney must be an advocate for a client. It is impossible to be an advocate for two parties with opposing interests.

It is not uncommon for one party to retain an attorney and for the other party not to do so. In such cases, the party with the attorney files for the divorce, and agreements reached between the parties are typically sent to the spouse for approval prior to any court hearing. Although it may feel like the attorney, by drafting the settlement documents, is representing both parties, it is simply not the case. The attorney owes a duty to the client to act solely in his or her best interest.

Do not let your spouse's assertions that you do not need an attorney, affect your decision. It will always serve you best to meet with a lawyer, and to obtain your own representation, even if it is only for advice on how proceeding without a lawyer could affect your legal rights.

3.6   What information should I take with me to the first meeting with my attorney?

Attorneys differ on the amount of information they like you to bring to an initial consultation. Make sure to ask the person with whom you schedule the initial consultation what documents you should bring. If you or your spouse has already initiated a court proceeding, such as a divorce or order of protection take copies of any court filings.

Other important documents you should bring include, prenuptial or postnuptial agreements, individual and business tax returns, tax related documents (W-2s, 1099s, and K-1s) recent pay stubs, recent account statements, and any appraisals you may have on real estate or other assets.

If your situation is urgent or you do not have access to these documents, do not let it stop you from scheduling appointments with the attorneys you are considering retaining.

Obtaining prompt legal advice early will likely prove more beneficial than having all of your important financial information available before your first consultation. Many clients have little to no access to many of the documents that will later prove critical to their divorce. Your attorney can explain to you the options for obtaining these financial records through the discovery process.

3.7 What unfamiliar words might an attorney use at the first meeting?

Law has a language all its own, and attorneys sometimes lapse into "legalese," forgetting that nonlawyers may not recognize words routinely used in the practice of law. Some words and phrases you might hear include:

- *Dissolution of marriage*—the divorce
- *Petitioner*—person who files the petition for dissolution of marriage
- *Respondent*—person who did not file the petition for dissolution of marriage
- *Jurisdiction*—authority of a court to make rulings affecting a party
- *Service*—process of notifying a party about a legal filing
- *Discovery*—process during which each side provides information to each other
- *Decree*—the final order entered in a divorce

Never hesitate to ask your attorney the meaning of a term. Your complete understanding of your lawyer's advice is essential for you to communicate effectively as possible.

3.8   What can I expect at an initial consultation with an attorney?

Initial consultations provide opportunities for both you and the attorney with whom you are meeting to determine whether or not entering into an attorney-client relationship makes sense under the circumstances—and whether or not there is a good fit. It is an opportunity for you to describe your current circumstances, express your concerns and ascertain whether you think an effective working relationship with the attorney will be possible. Likewise, the attorney will be making his or her own determinations about the nature of your case and whether he or she thinks that an effective attorney-client relationship might be established.

During the meeting, expect to ask a lot of questions and have questions asked of you. In general, you should be prepared to share the following information with the attorney:

- A brief history of the marriage
- Background information regarding yourself, your spouse, and your children
- Your immediate circumstances
- Your goals regarding custody, support, and property division
- What information you are seeking from the attorney during the consultation

You can expect the attorney to discuss the following topics with you:

- The procedure for divorce in Missouri
- A preliminary overview the issues in you case
- Background information about the firm
- Information about fees and filings

Understand that many questions may be impossible for the attorney to answer at the initial consultation because additional information or research is needed.

3.9   Will the communication with my attorney be confidential?

Yes. Your lawyer has an ethical duty to maintain confidentiality. This duty of confidentiality also extends to the paralegals and other support staff working with your attorney. The privileged information that you share with your attorney will remain private and confidential. However, you should be aware that the privilege could be waived by voluntary disclosing the communication to third parties.

3.10   Is there any way that I could unintentionally waive the attorney-client privilege, as it relates to the duty of confidentiality?

Yes. To ensure that communications between you and your attorney remain confidential, and to protect against the voluntary or involuntary waiver of such privilege, below are some tips to consider:

- Refrain from disclosing the content of the communications with your attorney, or discussing in substantive detail the communications with your attorney with third parties. Be aware that third parties include friends, family members, and all other individuals that are non-essential to the transmission of the communication. People that would qualify as essential to the transmission of the communication include, interpreters, court appointed guardians, and anyone appointed as a next-friend.

- Social media provides the potential for waiving the attorney-client privilege by publicly disclosing confidential information. Do not post information or send messages relating to your case on Facebook, Twitter, or other social media websites.

- Do not post information relating to your case or communications with your attorney on a personal blog, video blog, online chat rooms, or online message boards.

- Do not use your work related e-mail or any other e-mail account that third parties have the right to view without your permission to communicate with your attorney, or to discuss your case. Depending upon your employer's policy relating to electronic communication, the attorney-client privilege could potentially be waived by communicating with your attorney or by discussing your case through your personal e-mail account (G-mail, Yahoo, etc.) via a company computer. To ensure your communications remain confidential, it is best to only communicate via e-mail from your private e-mail address from your home computer.

3.11 Can I take a friend or family member to my initial consultation?

You will need to ask the attorney if he or she is amenable to having someone accompany you at the initial consultation. Although having someone present during your initial consultation can be a source of great support, the presence of this third party present will impact the attorney-client privilege.

There will not be any issues if your support person simply escorts you to and from the consultation. However, if you want this person to sit in on the consultation (and this is not uncommon) you should communicate this preference to the attorney ahead of time. If the attorney does not have an issue with your request, you might ask your support person take notes on your behalf so that you can focus on listening and asking questions.

3.12 What exactly will my attorney do to help me get a divorce?

Depending on the particulars of your case, your attorney may perform any of the following tasks on your behalf:

- Assess the relevant facts to determine proper jurisdiction and venue
- Advise you about all aspects of your divorce
- Prepare and file legal documents with the court
- Conduct discovery to obtain information from your spouse and other third parties, which might include depositions, requests for production of documents, requests for admissions, interrogatories, and subpoenas
- Appear with you at all court appearances, depositions, and conferences
- Support you in responding to information/discovery requests from your spouse's attorney

- Inform you of actions you are required to take
- Perform financial analyses of your case
- Locate appropriate experts to testify on your behalf if needed
- Conduct legal research and analysis
- Prepare you for court appearances and depositions
- Prepare your case for hearings and trial, including preparing exhibits and interviewing witnesses
- Advise you regarding your rights legal
- Offer guidance based upon experience throughout the case
- Counsel you regarding the risks and benefits of negotiated settlement as compared to proceeding to trial

As your advocate, your attorney is entrusted to take all of the steps necessary to represent your interests in the divorce.

3.13 What professionals should I expect to work with during my divorce?

Depending upon the issues identified by your attorney, you can expect to work with various types of professionals such as appraisers, financial professionals, accountants, vocational experts, and mental health experts.

Additionally, in some cases in which custody issues are seriously disputed or there have been allegations of abuse or neglect, the court will appoint a *guardian ad litem (GAL)*. The court will appoint a licensed Missouri lawyer to act as a GAL. He or she will represent the best interest of the child. A guardian *ad litem* has the responsibility to investigate you and your spouse as well as the needs of your child. She or he will act as the attorney on your child's behalf and will participate at trial, including calling witnesses and having the opportunity to examine the parties' witnesses. After the presentation of all evidence, the court will call upon the guardian to make custody and visitation recommendations to the court.

A psychologist is another expert whom the court could appoint to perform evaluations. The role of the psychologist will depend upon the specific purpose for which she or he was appointed. Most commonly, psychologists are appointed to perform child custody evaluations, which involve assessing both parents and the child. However, depending upon the circumstances, the court may order the psychologist to evaluate one parent to assess the child's safety while spending time with that parent.

3.14 I've been divorced before, and I don't think I need an attorney this time; however, my spouse is hiring one. Is it wise to go it alone?

Having gone through a prior divorce, it's likely that you gained a great deal of experience with the divorce process and may even have developed a basic understanding of Missouri divorce law. However, there are many reasons why proceeding without legal representation is likely a choice you will later regret. Every divorce is different. Differences such as the length of the marriage, the existence of children, the relative financial positions of you and your spouse, as well as your age and health can all impact the outcome of your divorce. Additionally, if your spouse hires an attorney, you will be at a distinct disadvantage with respect to many aspects of the case, including, drafting pleadings, testimonial motions, and court procedure among others.

Further, the law may have changed since your last divorce. Even if the divorce statutes have not been changed by the legislature, there will certainly have been appellate court opinions, that refine or limit the application of the relevant statutes. These appellate decisions are handed down by the Missouri Supreme Court and the three divisions of the Missouri Court of Appeals throughout the year and could potentially impact one or more issues in your divorce.

3.15 Can I take my children to meetings with my attorney?

It's best to make other arrangements for your children when you meet with your attorney. It will be helpful if you can give your full attention to your attorney and the issues you'll be discussing. Taking your child with you to your divorce attorney's office can add to your child's anxiety about the process. It can also open you up to criticism by your spouse.

Further, most law offices are not designed to accommodate young children and do not ordinarily have staff that can look after your children. In order to avoid exposing the children to these issues or otherwise involving them in the process, you should make the necessary plans for their care for the times you will be meeting with your attorney.

3.16 What is the role of the *paralegal* or *legal assistant* in my attorney's office?

A *paralegal,* or *legal assistant,* is a trained legal professional whose duties include providing support for you and your lawyer. Working with a paralegal can make your divorce easier because he or she is likely to be very available to help you. Making use of paralegals can also help to lower your legal costs, as the hourly rate for paralegal services is less than the rate for attorneys.

A paralegal is prohibited from giving legal advice. It is important that you respect the limits of the role of the paralegal if he or she is unable to answer your question because it calls for giving a legal opinion. However, a paralegal can answer many questions and provide a great deal of information to you throughout your divorce.

Paralegals can help you by receiving information from you, reviewing documents with you, providing you with updates on your case, and answering questions about the divorce process that do not call for legal advice.

3.17 My attorney is not returning my phone calls. What can I do?

It is a reasonable expectation to have your phone calls returned by your lawyer in a timely manner. What constitutes a timely manner may vary from time to time, depending upon whether the lawyer is in court or in depositions or other activity which takes the lawyer out of the office for significant blocks of time. Nevertheless, a returned call by the lawyer or someone on his or her behalf within about twenty-four hours is a reasonable expectation. If you are not receiving return calls, here are some options to address the situation:

- Ask to speak to the paralegal or another attorney in the office.
- Send an e-mail or fax telling your lawyer that you have been trying to reach him or her by phone and

explaining the reason it is important that you receive a call.

- Ask the receptionist to schedule a phone conference for you to speak with your attorney at a specific date and time.
- Schedule a meeting with your attorney to discuss both the issue needing attention as well as your concerns about the communication.

If your calls are not being returned, take action to get the communication with your lawyer back on track—most lawyers prefer to resolve client relationship issues when they first arise. However, if you continue to encounter difficulties, it may be time to consider finding new counsel.

3.18   How do I know when it's time to change lawyers?

Not all attorney-client engagements make it all the way to the conclusion of the divorce. There are many reasons why the relationship does not work, ranging from disagreement on strategy to non-payment for services. Regardless of the reason, if it becomes clear that you and your current attorney can no longer work together to bring the case to resolution, then a change of lawyer is needed.

Be aware that changing lawyers in the middle of the case raises several issues. First, you will incur legal fees for your new attorney to review information, which is already familiar to your current attorney. You also duplicate effort by explaining much of the same information to your new lawyer. A change in lawyers may also result in delays in the divorce.

The following are questions to ask yourself when you're deciding whether to stay with your attorney or seek new counsel:

- Have I spoken directly to my attorney about my concerns?
- When I expressed concerns, did my lawyer take action accordingly?
- Is my lawyer open and receptive to what I have to say?
- Am I blaming my lawyer for bad behavior of my spouse or opposing counsel?

- Have I provided my lawyer the information needed for taking the next action?
- Does my lawyer have control over the complaints I have, or do my complaints relate to the current law or the judge's determinations?
- Is my lawyer keeping promises for completing action on my case?
- Do I trust my lawyer?
- What would be the advantages of changing lawyers when compared to the cost?
- Do I believe my lawyer will support me to achieve the outcome I'm seeking in my divorce?

Reasonable effort should be made to resolve concerns with your attorney. If you have made this effort and the situation remains unchanged, it is a good indicator that the time has come to switch lawyers.

3.19 Are there certain expectations that I should have when working with my legal team?

Yes. Your legal team will be able to provide you with support and guidance throughout the divorce process. There are certain actions you can expect your legal team to do for you during your divorce. A list of some of them follows.

Meet with you prior to the filing of a court action to advise you on actions you should take first. There may be important steps to take before you initiate the legal process. Your legal team can support you to be well prepared prior to initiating divorce.

Take action to obtain a temporary court order or to enforce existing orders. Temporary court orders are often needed to ensure clarity regarding rights and responsibilities while your divorce is pending. Your legal team can help you obtain a temporary order and ask the court to enforce its orders if there is a violation.

Explain the legal process during each step of your case. Understanding the legal process reduces the stress of your divorce. Your legal team can guide you each step of the way.

Listen to your concerns and answer any questions. Although only the attorneys can give you legal advice, everyone on your team is available to listen, to provide support, and to direct you to the right person who can help.

Support you in developing your parenting plan. Many parents do not know how to decide what type of parenting plan is best for their children. Your legal team can help you look at the needs of you children and offer advice based on their experience in working with families.

Support you in the completion of your discovery responses and preparing for depositions. The discovery process can be overwhelming for anyone. You will be asked to provide detailed information and many documents. Your legal team can make this job easier. Just ask. If your case involves depositions, your legal team will support you to be fully prepared for the experience.

Identify important issues, analyze the evidence, and advise you. Divorce is complex. Often there is a great deal of uncertainty. Your legal team can analyze the unique facts of your case and advise you based upon the law and their expertise.

Communicate with the opposing party's attorney to try to resolve issues without going to court, and to keep your case progressing. Although your attorney cannot control the actions of the opposing party or their lawyer, your attorney can always initiate communication as your advocate. Phoning, e-mailing, or writing to opposing counsel are actions your legal team can take to encourage cooperation and to keep your divorce moving forward at the pace you want without the expense of contested litigation.

Think creatively regarding challenges with your case and provide options for your consideration. At the outset, you may see many obstacles to reach a final resolution. Your legal team can offer creative ideas for resolving challenges and help you to explore your options to achieve the best possible outcome.

Facilitate the settlement process. Although your legal team can never make the other party settle, your attorney can take action to promote settlement. They can prepare settlement proposals, invite settlement conferences, and negotiate zealously on your behalf.

3.20 Are there certain things my legal team will not be able to do?

Yes. Although there are many ways in which your legal team can support you during your divorce, there are also things your legal team will not be able to accomplish.

Force the other parent to exercise their parenting time. Your legal team cannot force a parent to exercise parenting time. However, be mindful that a chronic neglect of parenting time may be a basis for modifying your parenting plan. Tell your attorney if the other parent is repeatedly failing to exercise their parenting time.

Force the other party to respond to a settlement proposal. Your attorney may send proposals or make requests to opposing counsel; however, there is no duty to respond. After repeated follow-ups without a response, it may be clear no response is coming. At that time, your attorney will decide whether the issues merit court action. Both parties must agree on all terms for a case to be settled without a trial. If one party wants to proceed to trial, even over a single issue, he or she will be able to do so.

Control the tone of communication from opposing counsel or communications from the other party, or the other party's family members. Unfortunately, communication from the opposing attorney may sometimes appear rude, condescending, or demanding. Your legal team cannot stop an attorney from using these tactics.

Absent a pattern of harassment, your legal team cannot stop the other party or third parties from contacting you. If you do not want the contact, talk with your attorney about how to best handle the situation. Of course, appropriate communication regarding your children is always encouraged.

Ask the court to compensate you for every wrong done to you by the other party over the course of your marriage. Although your attorney will empathize that you do have valid complaints, please understand that focusing on the most important issues will yield the best outcome in the end. Raising numerous small issues may distract from your most important goal.

Remedy poor financial decisions made during the marriage. With few exceptions, the court's duty is to divide the marital estate, as it currently exists. The judge will not attempt to remedy all past financial wrongs, such as overspending or poor investments by your spouse. If there is significant debt, consult with a debt counselor or bankruptcy lawyer.

Control how the other party parents your children during his or her parenting time. Each parent has strengths and weaknesses. Absent special needs of a child, most judges will not issue orders regarding bedtimes, amount of TV watching or playing video games, discipline methods, clothing, or diet. Of course, any suspected abuse should be reported immediately to the appropriate authorities.

Leveraging money for rights regarding your children. Tactics oriented toward asserting custody rights as leverage toward attaining financial goals will be discouraged. Your legal team should negotiate parenting issues based solely on considerations related to your child, then, separately negotiate child support based on financial considerations.

Guarantee payment of child support and maintenance. Enforcement of payment of support is only possible when it is court ordered. However, even with a court order, you may experience inconsistent timing of payment due to job loss or a refusal to pay. Talk with your attorney if a pattern of repeated missed payments has developed.

Collect child care and uninsured medical expenses if provisions of the decree are not complied with. If your decree requires you to provide documentation of payment of expenses to the other party and you fail to, you could be prohibited from collecting reimbursement for those expenses.

Follow the court's orders regarding providing documentation to the other parent, even if they don't pay as they should. Always keep records of these expenses and payments made by each parent, and keep copies of communications with the other parent regarding payment/reimbursement. It is much easier to keep these records on an ongoing basis than to get copies of old checks, day care bills, medical bills and insurance documents at a later time.

4

Attorney Fees and Costs

Anytime you make a major investment, you want to know what the cost is going to be and what you are getting for your money. Investing in quality legal representation for your divorce is no different. The legal expenses for your divorce might be one of your primary concerns. Your desire to maximize the value of your legal dollar makes you an intelligent consumer of legal services. Although you do not want to sacrifice quality, you should endeavor to secure the best value for the fees you are paying.

Legal fees for a divorce can be costly and the total expense is usually not predictable. However, there are many actions you can take to manage and reduce the costs. Develop a plan early on for how you will finance your divorce. Speak openly with your lawyer about fees from the outset. Learn as much as you can about how you will be charged. By being informed, aware, and wise, your financial investment in your divorce will be money well spent to protect your future.

4.1 Can I get free legal advice from a lawyer over the phone?

Although the majority of family law attorneys will be more than glad to speak to potential clients in general terms, you should not expect to receive free legal advice. Most questions about your divorce are too complex for a lawyer to give a meaningful answer during a brief phone call. Questions about your divorce require a thorough review of the facts, circumstances, and background of your marriage. To obtain good legal advice, it's best to schedule an initial consultation with a lawyer who handles divorces.

4.2 Will I be charged for an initial consultation with a lawyer?

It depends. Some lawyers provide free initial consultations, while others charge a fee or employ a "hybrid arrangement" of some kind. When scheduling your appointment, the firm should inform you about any consultation fees. If the information is not offered, you should inquire so that you will know what to expect when you arrive for your consultation.

4.3 If I decide to hire an attorney, when do I have to pay him or her?

If your attorney charges for an initial consultation, be prepared to make payment at the time of your meeting. At the close of your consultation, the attorney may tell you the amount of the retainer needed by the law firm to handle your divorce. However, you are not generally expected to pay the retainer at the time of your first meeting. Rather, the retainer is paid after the lawyer has accepted your case, you have decided to hire the lawyer, and you are ready to proceed.

4.4 What exactly is a *retainer* and how much will mine be?

A *retainer* is a sum paid to your lawyer in advance for services to be performed and costs to be incurred in your divorce. This will be either an amount paid toward a "flat fee" for your divorce or an advance credit for services that will be charged by the hour.

If the law firm accepts your case, expect the attorney to request a retainer following the initial consultation. The amount of the retainer may vary, but realistically one should be prepared to commit to the payment of a few thousand to many thousands of dollars, depending upon the nature and complexity of your case. Examples of issues that are all likely to require higher retainers include custody disputes, ownership of non-publicly traded businesses, complex tracing of separate property, and interstate disputes.

Additionally, it is not uncommon for a different attorney that you hire to represent you after you have terminated your relationship with a prior attorney to charge a higher retainer, especially in situations where the court had already set a trial date. A larger advance payment may be required because, under these circumstances, the attorney will need to expend substantial up-front effort over a very limited period of time.

4.5 Will my attorney accept my divorce case on a contingency-fee basis?

No. A contingency fee is one that only becomes payable if your case is successful. In Missouri, lawyers are ethically prohibited from entering into a contingent-fee contract in any divorce case. Your lawyer cannot accept payment based upon securing your divorce, the amount of maintenance or support awarded, or the division of the property settlement.

4.6 How much does it cost to get a divorce?

This question has no simple answer. The amount you will pay in legal expenses for your divorce will depend upon numerous factors, many of which will be unknown at the time you hire an attorney. The vast majority of Missouri family law attorneys charge by the hour. This is because your attorney cannot know how much time and effort your case will require at the outset. Although some attorneys charge for divorces using a flat fee (a fixed amount for the legal services being provided), these are more likely to be used when there are no children and the parties are already in agreement upon the division of their property and debts.

It is important that you discuss the cost of your divorce before you engage an attorney. If you and your attorney are not on the same page regarding the realities of the costs, conflicts may soon arise.

As discussed above, most family law attorneys will request a retainer, or a fee advance, prior to beginning work on your case. Be sure to ask your attorney what portion, if any, of the retainer is refundable if you do not continue with the case or if you terminate your relationship with the attorney.

4.7 What are typical hourly rates for a divorce lawyer?

Hourly rates vary throughout Missouri, and attorneys who practice in the divorce area may charge from $150 per hour to more than three times that rate. Rates also tend to vary based upon location, and attorneys in St. Louis, Kansas City, Springfield and Columbia/Jefferson City metropolitan areas may charge more per hour than their counterparts in less densely populated areas. The variability of hourly rates is attributable to factors such as skill, reputation, experience, overhead costs in the geographic area in which the attorney practices, and exclusive focus on divorce law.

4.8 If I can't afford to pay the full amount of the retainer, can I make monthly payments to my attorney?

Each law firm makes these types of determinations on a case-by-case basis. Frequently, a person's inability to pay the initial retainer indicates to an attorney that he or she may have difficulty getting paid as the case progresses. Make sure to let prospective attorneys know if your inability to pay the full amount of the retainer stems from the fact that your spouse has complete control of the assets. An attorney is more likely to accept your case without a retainer or with a reduced retainer if it is clear to him or her that there are sufficient funds in the marital estate, but the those funds are presently inaccessible.

In cases such as this, the attorney can file a motion to request payment of attorney's fees while the case is pending. In other circumstances, it may be that a person's inability to pay the retainer reflects the need to seek other, more affordable counsel.

4.9 I agreed to pay my attorney a substantial retainer to begin my case. Will I still have to make monthly payments?

Be certain to ask all questions you have regarding billing with your attorney prior to signing the engagement letter. Clarify with your attorney what will be expected of you regarding payments on your account while the divorce is in progress. Although there is no uniform practice, most attorneys will require you to pay for the services they provide on a monthly basis. After the advance payment has been exhausted, the attorney may require you to replace it with another such payment, or simply pay the outstanding balance each month.

Attorneys have only their time to offer, and there are only so many hours in a day. Just like professionals in every other field, attorneys expect to get paid for the work that they perform. If you do not agree, you are likely to face issues at some point during the representation. Many fee agreements include provisions for an attorney's withdrawal from your case in the event of nonpayment.

4.10 My lawyer gave me an estimate of the cost of my divorce and it sounds reasonable. Do I still need a written fee agreement?

Absolutely. An estimate represents nothing more than an educated guess. There are numerous factors that cannot be known by your attorney before the representation begins which may substantially alter any good faith estimate. A written agreement will not only define the scope of the services for which you have hired your lawyer, but will also to memorialize key aspects of the representation, including your attorney's hourly rate, whether you will be billed for certain costs such as copying, and when you can expect to receive statements on your account.

A clear fee agreement reduces the risk of misunderstandings between you and your lawyer. It supports you both in being clear about your promises to one another so that your focus can be on the legal services being provided rather than on disputes about your fees.

4.11 How will I know how the fees and charges are accumulating?

Your fee agreement should address the manner and frequency of charges incurred. Most fee agreements will likely already include provisions detailing their billing, hourly rates, and costs. If any fee agreement you receive does not include provisions for these items, you should insist that they be added. It is perfectly reasonable to ask that your attorney provide monthly statements which include a detailed listing of the charges incurred.

Review the statement of your account promptly after you receive it. Check to make sure there are no errors. If your statement reflects work that you were unaware was performed, call for clarification. Your attorney's office should welcome any questions you have about services it provided.

Your statement might also include expenses such as filing fees, court reporter fees, copy expenses, research fees, or interest charged on your account, if unpaid balances accrue interest per your fee agreement. If more than a month has passed since your last statement on your account, call your attorney's office to request one. Legal fees can mount quickly, and it is important that you stay aware of the status of your legal expenses.

4.12 What other expenses are related to the divorce litigation besides lawyer fees?

As with most everything relating to divorce, the answer to this question will depend on your case. Throughout the course of the case, there will be associated expenses. These expenses fall into three categories: mandatory, administrative, and elective.

- *Mandatory expenses* are typically ordered by the court or are associated with a mandatory court program. Examples of mandatory expenses include the initial filing fee, parent education classes mandated by some, but not all, jurisdictions, guardian *ad litem* fees (if one is appointed by the court).

- *Administrative expenses* include items such as copying and legal research.

- *Elective expenses* encompass those expenses which you elect to incur to further your case. A few examples include fees for expert witnesses or special process servers to serve initial pleadings and/or subpoenas. It may also include court reporters fees for deposition appearances and transcript preparation.

Unless your fee agreement specifies to the contrary, you should expect that there will be expenses for which you will be responsible over and above your attorney's hourly charges. Speak with your attorney throughout your case regarding upcoming extra expenses so that they do not come as a surprise. Also, discuss the costs other than attorney fees that may arise, given the complexities of your case.

Although not every case requires expert witnesses, in those that do, the expert-witness fees can be a substantial expense, ranging from hundreds to thousands of dollars. Attorneys utilize expert witnesses in divorce cases for many different reasons including, valuing privately held businesses, tracing separate property, calculating tax consequences, appraising real estate, and determining employability, among many others.

Speak frankly with your attorney about these costs so that together you can make the best decisions about how to use your budget for the litigation.

4.13 Who pays for the experts such as appraisers, accountants, psychologists, and mediators?

Whether appointed by the court or hired by the spouses, the parties themselves ordinarily pay for costs for the services of experts. In the case of the guardian *ad litem*, who may be appointed to represent the best interest of your children, the amount of the fee will depend upon how much time this professional spends. The judge often orders this fee to be shared by the parties. However, depending upon the circumstances, one party can be ordered to pay the entire fee. If you can demonstrate *indigency,* that is, a very low income and no ability to pay, the county may be ordered to pay your share of the guardian ad *litem* fee.

Psychologists charge either by the hour or set a flat fee for a certain type of evaluation. Again, the court can order one party to pay this fee or both parties to share the expense. It is not uncommon for a psychologist to request payment in advance and hold the release of an expert report until fees are paid.

Mediators either charge a flat fee per session or an hourly rate. Generally, each party will pay one-half of the mediator's fees, which is paid prior to your mediation sessions.

The fees for many experts, including appraisers and accountants, will vary depending upon whether the individuals are called upon to provide only a specific service such as an appraisal, or whether they will need to prepare for giving testimony and appear as a witness at trial.

4.14　What factors will impact how much my divorce will cost?

Although it is difficult to predict how much your legal fees will be, the following are some of the factors that affect the cost:

- Whether there are children
- Whether child custody is agreed upon
- Whether there are novel legal questions
- Whether a pension plan will be divided between the parties
- The nature of the issues contested
- The number of issues agreed to by the parties
- The cooperation of the opposing party and opposing counsel
- The frequency of your communication with your legal team
- The ability of the parties to communicate with each other, as well as the client's ability to communicate with her attorney
- The promptness with which information is provided and/or exchanged between both the clients and the attorneys
- Whether there are litigation costs, such as fees for expert witnesses or court reporters
- The hourly rate of the attorney
- The time it will take to conclude your divorce

Communicating with your lawyer regularly about your legal fees will help you to have a better understanding of the overall cost as your case proceeds.

4.15　Will my attorney charge for phone calls and e-mails?

Unless your case is being handled on a flat-fee basis or you have worked out a different arrangement in your fee agreement, you should expect to be charged for any communication with your attorney. Many of the professional services provided by lawyers are done by phone and by e-mail. This time can be spent giving legal advice, negotiation, or gathering information to protect your interests. These calls and e-mails are all legal services for which you should anticipate being charged by your attorney.

To make the most efficient use of your time during attorney phone calls, plan your call in advance. Organize the information you want to relay, your questions, and any concerns to be addressed. This will help you to be clear and focused during the phone call so that your fees are well spent.

4.16 Will I be charged for talking to the staff at my lawyer's office?

The answer depends on the terms provided in your fee agreement. Check the terms of your fee agreement with your lawyer. Prior to having your attorney start work on your case, you should have a clear understanding as to whose time you will be charged for and at what rate they are charging. Whether you are charged fees for talking to nonlawyer members of the law office may depend upon their role in the office. For example, many law firms charge for the services of paralegals and law clerks.

Remember that the lawyer or law firm you are working with has staff for a reason. Under the supervision of an attorney, a paralegal or secretary can perform important tasks more efficiently and economically than the attorney. Because the hourly rate the law firm charges for staff is substantially less than that of the attorney, having the staff perform those functions best suited to their abilities represents a significant cost savings.

It is important to remember that nonlawyers are prohibited from giving legal advice or opinions. Accordingly, they will defer all such inquiries to the attorneys on your case. Staff will however, will be able relay your messages and receive information from you. They may also be able to answer many of your questions.

4.17 What is a *litigation budget,* and how do I know if I need one?

If your case is complex and you are anticipating substantial legal fees, ask your attorney to prepare a *litigation budget* for your review. This can help you to understand the nature of the services anticipated, the time that may be spent, and the overall amount it will cost to proceed to trial. The litigation budget will likely be comprised of a combination of your attorney and your legal team's hourly rates. It can also be helpful for budgeting and planning for additional retainers. Knowing the anticipated costs of litigation can help you to make meaningful decisions about which issues to litigate and which to consider resolving through settlement negotiations.

4.18 What is a *trial retainer* and will I have to pay one?

A *trial retainer* is an agreed upon amount of money paid to your attorney in anticipation of the expenses associated with both the preparation of your case for trial and the trial itself. The purpose of the trial retainer is to fund the work needed to prepare for trial and for services the day or days of trial. A trial retainer is a sum of money paid on your account with your lawyer when it appears as though your case may not settle by a negotiated agreement, and is at risk for proceeding to trial.

Starting approximately sixty to ninety days prior to your trial setting, you should expect both the activity level surrounding to your case to significantly increase. In order to make sure that these expenses are covered, your attorney may ask you for a trial retainer. Many fee agreements provide that a trial retainer may be sought in this circumstance.

Confirm with your attorney that any unearned portion of your trial retainer will be refunded if your case settles. Ask your lawyer whether and when a trial retainer might be required in your case so that you can avoid surprises and plan your budget accordingly.

4.19 How do I know whether I should spend the attorney fees my lawyer says it will require to take my case to trial?

Settlement of a case requires the agreement of both sides. When one side remains unreasonable and refuses to engage in meaningful settlement discussions you really do not have a choice but to proceed to trial. Even when the other side has its last, best offer on the table, you will need to consider that offer in light of the range of possible outcomes at trial. If, after consulting with your attorney, you believe that you will do better than your spouse's best offer plus the cost of a trial, it makes economic sense to proceed to trial. However, when your spouse's best offer falls somewhere within the range of possible trial outcomes you must decide if the possibility of doing better at trial is worth the risk of doing worse.

Unlike other types of civil litigation, a divorce settlement involves numerous issues including division of property, spousal maintenance, custody, and child support. Because all of these issues intertwine and impact upon the others it is frequently difficult to settle individual issues if the parties cannot reach a full settlement. Deciding whether to take a case to trial or to settle is often the most challenging point in the divorce process. This decision should be made with the guidance and support of your attorney.

Frequently in divorce cases, the most significant attorneys fees and expenses are incurred in the weeks leading up to trial. In addition to general trial preparation, the attorney must update all financial information, issue trial subpoenas, coordinate the attendance of the expert witnesses and prepare trial exhibits. You should not neglect to consider the additional and substantial costs of trial preparations and trial in determining whether to proceed to trial.

When the issues in dispute are primarily financial, often the decision about settlement is related to the cost of a trial. Determine just how far apart you and your spouse are on the financial matters, and compare this to the estimated costs of going to trial. By comparing these amounts, you can decide whether a compromise on certain financial issues and certainty about the outcome would be better than paying legal fees and not knowing how your case will resolve.

4.20   Is there any way I can reduce some of the expenses of getting a divorce?

Litigation of any kind can be expensive, and divorces are no exception. While there will be certain costs over which you have little control, there are also many ways that you can help to keep expenses down. These include:

Put it in writing. If you need to relay information that is important but not urgent, consider providing it to your attorney by mail, fax, or e-mail. This creates a prompt and accurate record for your file and takes less time than exchanging phone messages and talking on the phone. Also, unless you require a timely response, hold off on sending separate e-mails for each of the questions that cross your mind throughout the course of a day. By sending multiple questions in one e-mail as opposed many e-mails throughout the day, your attorney can focus all of his or her attention on your case at one time and will generally spend less time doing so.

Discuss more than one matter during a call. It is not unusual for clients to have many questions during litigation. When you address these questions in telephone calls with your attorney, consider waiting to call until you have more than one inquiry.

Keep your attorney informed. Just as your attorney should keep you up to date on the status of your case, you need to do the same. Keep your lawyer apprised about any major developments in your life such as changes to your employment status, major unexpected expenses or changes in your health.

Also make sure to notify your attorney, if your contact information changes. Your attorney may need to reach you with information, and reaching you in a timely manner may help avoid more costly fees later.

Obtain copies of documents. An important part of litigation includes reviewing documents such as tax returns, account statements, report cards, or medical records. Your attorney will ordinarily be able to request or subpoena these items, but many may be readily available to you directly upon request.

Consult your attorney's website. If your lawyer has a website, it may be a great source of useful information. The answers to commonly asked questions about the divorce process can often be found there.

Utilize support professionals. Get to know the support staff at your lawyer's office. Although only attorneys are able to give you legal advice, the receptionist, paralegal, legal secretary, or law clerk may be able to answer generic questions such as the status of certain documents or due dates. Your engagement letter with the attorney should specify the hourly rates charge by the attorney's staff members. Just as with your communication with your attorney, all communication with any professionals in a law firm is required to be kept strictly confidential.

Consider working with an associate attorney. Although the senior attorneys or partners in a law firm may have more experience, you may find that working with an associate attorney, individually or under the supervision of a senior attorney, is a good option. Hourly rates for an associate attorney are typically lower than those charged by a senior partner. Frequently the associate attorney has trained under a senior partner and developed excellent skills as well as knowledge of the law.

Discuss with the firm the benefits of working with a senior or an associate attorney in light of the nature of your case, the expertise of the respective attorneys, and the potential cost savings to you.

Provide timely responses to information requests. Whenever possible, provide information requested by your lawyer in a timely manner. This avoids the cost of follow-up action by your lawyer and the additional expense of extending the time in litigation.

Carefully review your monthly statements. Scrutinize your monthly billing statements closely. If you believe an error has been made, contact your lawyer's office right away to discuss your concerns. Your attorney should have no problem explaining his or her bill or fixing any billing errors that appear on your statement.

Make rational economic decisions. Understand that when your disagreements concern a financial matter, the amount in dispute may be less than the amount it would cost to fight the issue. By making economically rational decisions, you can use your legal fees wisely and help to control the costs of your divorce.

4.21 I don't have any money and I need a divorce. What are my options?

If you have a low income and few assets, you may elect to represent yourself in court. Some Missouri judicial districts have special court sessions for divorce cases in which individuals are representing themselves. You might also consider the following options:

- Contact one of the Missouri Legal Services offices (Legal Services of Eastern Missouri, Legal Services of

Western Missouri, Mid-Missouri Legal Services and Legal Services of Southern Missouri).

- Contact a local firm to see if they offer any *pro bono* services and if so to see if you qualify.
- Contact the Children and Family Advocacy Legal Clinic at Washington University School of Law, the Child and Family Services Clinic and the University of Missouri Kansas City (UMKC), as well as the legal clinics at the University of Missouri Columbia School of Law and Saint Louis University School of Law.

These organizations have a screening process for potential clients, as well as limits on the nature of the cases they take. The demand for their services is also usually greater than the number of attorneys available to handle cases. Consequently, if you are eligible for legal services from one of these programs, you should anticipate being on a waiting list.

In short, if you have very little income and few assets, you are likely to experience some delay in obtaining a lawyer. If you believe you might be eligible for participation in one of these programs, inquire early to increase your opportunity to get the legal help you are seeking.

4.22. I don't have much money, but I need to get a divorce as quickly as possible. What should I do?

If you have some money and want to divorce as soon as possible, consider some of these options:

- Borrow the legal fees from friends or family. Often those close to you are concerned about your future and would be pleased to support you in your goal of having your rights protected. Although this may be uncomfortable to do, remember that most people will appreciate that you trusted them enough to ask for their help. If the retainer is too much money to request from a single individual, consider whether a handful of persons might each be able to contribute a lesser amount to help you reach your goal of hiring a lawyer.
- Charge the legal fees on a low-interest credit card or consider taking out a loan.

- Start saving. If your case is not urgent, consider developing a plan for saving the money you need to proceed with a divorce. Your attorney may be willing to receive and hold monthly payments until you have paid an amount sufficient to pay the initial retainer.
- Talk to your attorney about using money held in a joint account with your spouse.
- Find an attorney who will work with you on a monthly payment basis.
- Ask your attorney about your spouse paying for your legal fees
- Ask your attorney about being paid from the proceeds of the property settlement. If you and your spouse have acquired substantial assets during the marriage, you may be able to find an attorney who will wait to be paid until the assets are divided at the conclusion of the divorce.

Closely examine all sources of funds readily available to you, as you may have overlooked money that might be easily accessible to you.

Even if you do not have the financial resources to proceed with your divorce at this time, consult with an attorney to learn your rights and to develop an action plan for steps you can take between now and the time you are able to proceed. Often there are measures you can take right away to protect yourself until you have the money to proceed with your divorce.

4.23 If a third party, such as a relative, pays my legal fees, will my lawyer give him or her private information about my divorce?

The fact that a third party has agreed to pay your legal fees does not make that individual the client. Your attorney owes his or her duty of confidentiality to you alone. Unless you authorize your attorney to communicate with the person paying your legal expenses, your lawyer is ethically bound not to disclose the details your case to anyone else.

Before you make any such authorizations, you should be aware that your attorney's communications with non-clients are not protected by any privilege and may be subject to discovery. Also, be aware that unless your fee agreement states differently, you will be charged for communications between your attorney and authorized parties. Regardless of the opinions and or instructions of the person who pays your attorney fees, your lawyer's duties are owed to you and you alone.

4.24 Can I ask the court to order my spouse to pay my attorney fees?

Yes. In order to obtain attorney's fees from your spouse, you must do so with a formal request. This request may be made in your petition or in a separate motion for fees. The fact that Missouri law allows you to request that your spouse pay some or all of your legal expenses does not relieve you of your payment obligations in the fee agreement. The trial court has a wide degree of discretion in awarding attorney's fees and no attorney can guarantee that you will be awarded fees, or if you are awarded fees, how much the fees will be.

If your case is likely to require costly experts and your spouse has a much greater ability to pay these expenses than you, talk to your lawyer about the possibility of filing a motion with the court asking your spouse to pay toward these costs while the case is pending.

4.25 What happens if I don't pay my attorney the fees I promised to pay?

The ethical rules for lawyers allow your attorney to seek to withdraw from representing you if do not comply with the terms of your fee agreement. In addition to withdrawing, your attorney may also assert a statutory attorney's lien and obtain a judgment on that lien against any property awarded to you in your divorce case. Alternatively, your attorney may file suit against you for any outstanding attorney's fees or costs owed to the firm. No lawyer enjoys having to withdraw, assert a lien against or sue a former client.

However, the legal field is no different than any service industry in this respect. Just as you would not expect a contractor to continue working on your home if you fail to pay as agreed, you cannot reasonably expect anything different from your attorney.

Should you experience difficulty paying your attorney's fees, open a dialogue with your attorney and discuss your options. Ask your attorney about different options, including payment plans. You may also consider borrowing the funds, using your credit card, or asking for help from friends and family.

Avoiding communication with your attorney when issues, such as inability to pay arise, will only further complicate the situation. To the attorney, it appears that they have a client that is not only not paying them, but also refusing to communicate. Without ongoing communication with you, it becomes more and more likely that your relationship will breakdown.

5

The Discovery Process

Discovery is one of the least talked about steps in divorce, but it is often among the most important. *Discovery* occurs in the pretrial phase of a lawsuit and is best described as a process through which each party may request and obtain evidence relevant to the divorce from the opposing party as well as third parties. The purpose of discovery is to give both you and your spouse the opportunity to access information that you each need to properly analyze all of the issues in the divorce. In this way, you can either negotiate a mutually agreeable settlement based upon all relevant facts, or have all of the facts and documents you need to present to the judge at trial.

The discovery process may seem tedious at times because of the need to obtain and to provide a lot of detailed information. Completing it, however, can provide tremendous clarity about the issues in your divorce. Trust your lawyer's advice about the importance of having the necessary evidence as you complete the discovery process in order to reach your goals in your divorce.

5.1 What types of discovery might be done by my lawyer or my spouse's lawyer?

There are several discovery tools available for the attorneys to gather the information that they require to properly analyze your case and prepare for trial, if necessary. The most common types of discovery include:

- *Interrogatories*—these are written questions submitted by one party to the other that must be answered under oath.

- *Requests for production of documents*—these are written requests submitted by one party to the other that request that certain documents be provided or produced for inspection.

- *Request for entry upon land for inspection*—these are written requests submitted by one party to allow the requesting party to gain access to specified property so that they may inspect, measure, survey, photograph and/or appraise the property itself or other items located on the property.

- *Requests for admissions*—these are written statements submitted by one party to the other that must either be admitted or denied.

- *Subpoena of documents*—these are formal documents issued by the clerk of the court that are served upon the individual or entity from whom documents are desired. The subpoena commands the recipient to appear at a designated time and place and produce the documents requested by the subpoena.

- *Depositions*—is a process whereby the persons being deposed answer questions posed to them by the parties' attorneys under oath in the presence of a court reporter but outside the presence of a judge. The court reporter prepares a transcript of everything that is said.

Each divorce case is unique. Many factors specific to your case can influence the type of discovery your attorney deems necessary to employ. These factors can include:

- The specific issues in dispute
- How much access you and your spouse have to needed information
- The level of cooperation in participating in *informal discovery* (voluntary exchange of information)
- The level of trust of your spouse and his or her attorney
- The budget available for performing discovery

Talk to your lawyer about the nature and extent of discovery anticipated in your case.

5.2   How long does the discovery process take?

Discovery can take anywhere from a few weeks to a number of months, depending upon the complexity of the case, the cooperation between you and your spouse, and whether expert witnesses are involved.

The *Missouri Rules of Civil Procedure* provide that interrogatories, requests for production of documents, and requests for admissions be responded to within thirty days. However, each party that has responded to any of these discovery devices has a duty to supplement their responses in a timely manner should their prior responses become inaccurate at a later date. For example, if at the beginning of the case you respond to an interrogatory that asks for the identity of your expert witnesses by stating that you have not retained an expert, you must provide and updated response when you do retain an expert.

Divorce cases are unlike other types of civil litigation when it comes to discovery. In most personal injury cases all of the relevant events over which the parties conduct discovery occurred in the past. In divorce, past, present, and future events impact the case. Bank and other financial accounts have constantly changing balances, and parties continue to receive assets in the form of salary, bonuses, and other types of deferred compensation. Your attorney must keep up with all of these things in order to maintain the most current and accurate picture of you and your spouse's financial situation.

5.3   My lawyer insists that we conduct discovery, but I don't want to spend the time and money on it. Is it really necessary?

The discovery process will be critical to a successful outcome in your case for several reasons:

- It increases the likelihood that any agreements reached are based on accurate, up-to-date information.
- It gives you access to the information necessary to make an informed decision regarding whether to settle or proceed to trial.

- It gives you access to important documents that may be evidence at trial.
- It helps to avoid surprises at trial, such as unexpected evidence or witness testimony.
- It gives your attorney access to the information he or she will need to address the disputed issues in your case.

Discuss with your attorney the rationale behind the discovery being conducted in your case to ensure it is tailored to your needs, consistent with your personal goals, and a meaningful investment of your legal fees.

5.4 I just received from my spouse's attorney interrogatories and requests that I produce documents. My lawyer wants me to respond within two weeks. I'll never make the deadline. What can I do?

Start work on responding immediately. Answering your discovery promptly will help move your case forward and help minimize your legal fees. There are steps you can take to make this task easier.

First, look at all of the questions. Many of them may not apply, or may only require simple "yes" or "no" answers.

See if your attorney or a member of the attorney's staff can help you. It is important that you develop the practice of letting others help you while you are going through your divorce. Chances are that you will make great progress in just a couple of hours with some assistance.

Break the discovery down into smaller tasks. If you answer just a few questions a day, the job will not be so overwhelming.

If you still think that you will not be able to meet the deadline, call your lawyer. It is not uncommon to request short extensions either informally from the opposing attorney or formally in a motion with the court. Unless there are time sensitive issues or there has been a repeated pattern of untimely responses, it is likely that your attorney will be able to secure some additional time. However, it is best not to make a habit of requesting extensions as delays in the discovery process often leads to frustration by clients and lawyers. Do your best to provide the information in a timely manner with the help of others.

5.5 **I don't have access to my documents and my spouse is being uncooperative in providing my lawyer with information. Can my lawyer request information directly from an employer or financial institution?**

Yes. Lawyers frequently issue subpoenas directly to employers, financial institutions, and other entities that possess relevant information. A *subpoena* is a court order directing an individual or corporate representative to appear before the court or to produce documents in a pending lawsuit. In the discovery process, a subpoena is used to compel an individual or corporation to produce documents, papers, books, or other physical exhibits that constitute or contain evidence that is relevant to your case.

5.6 **My spouse's lawyer intends to subpoena my medical records. Aren't these private?**

Ordinarily, your medical records are confidential and not subject to discovery. However, your medical information may be relevant in your divorce if you have a condition that impacts your ability to parent or your ability to work. Given the private and confidential nature of the information contained in your medical records, the court should limit discovery to only those medical conditions raised by the issues in your divorce. Talk with your lawyer about your rights. There are a number of options available to limit the disclosure of your information.

5.7 **I own my business, will I have to disclose my business records?**

Yes. The value of your business, and whether it is marital property or your separate property, is relevant to the divorce. If requested in discovery, you, or your company will be required to provide extensive records related to your business. Due to the sensitive nature of some business records, you will have the ability to file a motion requesting the implementation of a confidentiality or protective order. Make sure to let your attorney know the importance of protecting corporate documents so that he or she may take the necessary steps to do so.

5.8 **It's been two months since my lawyer sent interrogatories to my spouse, and we still don't have his answers. I answered mine on time. Is there anything that can be done to speed up the process?**

The failure or refusal of a spouse to follow the rules of discovery can add to both the frustration and expense of the divorce process. Talk with your attorney about filing a *motion to compel,* seeking a court order that your spouse provides the requested information by a certain date. A request for attorney fees for the filing of the motion may also be appropriate.

Ask your lawyer whether a subpoena of information from an employer or a financial institution would be a more cost effective way to get needed facts and documents if your spouse remains uncooperative.

5.9 **What is a *deposition*?**

A *deposition* is a means of discovery whereby the attorney asks questions of a witness while that person is under oath, in the presence of a court reporter. A deposition may be taken of you, your spouse, or potential witnesses in your divorce case, including experts. Both attorneys will be present. You and your spouse also have the right to be present during the taking of depositions of any witnesses in your case. If the person being deposed is not one of the parties, he or she will have the right to have his or her attorney present as well.

The court reporter takes down everything that is said at the deposition other than comments that the attorneys agree will be "off the record." Sometime after the deposition has concluded, the court reporter will transcribe the record and provide written copies to the attorneys. The person who was deposed has the right to elect to waive his or her right to review the transcript prepared by the court reporter for accuracy. Your attorney will discuss this choice with you at or before your deposition. If you elect not to waive, you will have an opportunity, before the transcript becomes final, to make corrections to the transcript. The corrections will be added to an "errata" sheet to the end of the deposition, and become part of the record.

Depositions most frequently are taken at the office of one of the parties' attorneys, but also may take place at a business or other mutually agreed upon location.

Depositions are not performed in every divorce. They are more common in cases involving contested custody, complex financial issues, and expert witnesses.

5.10 What is the purpose of a deposition?

Depositions serve several purposes, including:

- As an information gathering tool
- They allow your attorney to evaluate how witnesses will perform at trial.
- They allow your attorney to commit a witness to a specific position or opinion in the case.
- They give your attorney a means to impeach a witness at trial if their trial testimony conflicts with their deposition testimony.
- They help to eliminate surprises at the trial by learning the testimony of witnesses in advance, and possibly narrow the issues in the dispute.
- They preserve testimony of a witness in the event the witness becomes unavailable for trial.

Depositions can be essential tools in a divorce, especially when a case is likely to proceed to trial.

5.11 Will what I say in my deposition be used against me when we go to court?

Potentially. If your testimony at trial conflicts with your deposition testimony, you should expect that your spouse's attorney would use your deposition testimony to impeach you, by demonstrating the inconsistency. However, more often than not, a deposition is used to develop trial strategy and obtain information in preparation for trial. Your spouse's attorney will rely on testimony at trial by asking you those questions on cross-examination that elicit the information he or she wants the court to know.

5.12   Will the judge read the depositions?

Maybe. Although deposition transcripts are not filed with the court like motions or financial affidavits, there is no prohibition against using a deposition as a trial exhibit. If a witness becomes unavailable for trial or it appears there may limited trial time, your attorney may utilize a deposition transcript, or some portion thereof, as a trial exhibit.

5.13   How should I prepare for my deposition?

The first thing you should do to prepare for your deposition is to review the important documents in your case, such as the petition, counter-petition, answers to interrogatories, both parties' financial affidavits, and any temporary hearing affidavits. Ask your attorney if there are other important documents you should review prior to the deposition.

You should also schedule a meeting with your attorney in advance of the deposition to prepare you for what to expect. During this meeting your attorney can tell you the subjects over which you should expect to be questioned as well as what he or she knows about the other attorney's style or approach. You should bring up those subjects you are concerned about and discuss the best way to answer difficult questions. One of the best ways to prepare for your deposition is to have your attorney question you as if he or she was your spouse's attorney. This kind of "mock deposition" will give you a good idea of what to expect in your actual deposition.

5.14   What will I be asked? Can I refuse to answer questions?

Questions in a deposition can cover a broad range of topics including your education, work, income, and family. An attorney is allowed to ask you about anything that is reasonably calculated to lead to the discovery of admissible evidence. If the question may lead to relevant information, it can be asked in a deposition, even though it may be inadmissible at trial.

Your attorney may object to inappropriate questions. If there is an objection, say nothing until the attorneys discuss the objection. If you are unsure whether to answer a question, follow your lawyer's advice. Your lawyer may instruct you not to answer any question he or she believes to be impermissible.

5.15   What if I give incorrect information in my deposition?

You are required to tell the truth in your deposition and any time you testify. You will be under oath during your deposition, so it is very important that you be truthful. If you give incorrect information by mistake, contact your attorney as soon as you realize the error. If you lie during your deposition, you violate your oath to tell the truth and risk being impeached by the other lawyer during your divorce trial. This will almost certainly cause you to lose credibility with the court, rendering your testimony less valuable. The court expects both parties to tell the truth and the law demands it.

5.16   What if I don't know or can't remember the answer to a question?

You may be asked questions about which you have no knowledge. It is always acceptable to say "I don't know" if you do not have the knowledge. Similarly, if you cannot remember, simply say so.

5.17   What else do I need to know about having my deposition taken?

The following suggestions are intended help you to give a successful deposition:

- Prepare for your deposition by reviewing and providing necessary documents and talking with your lawyer in enough time in advance that you do not feel rushed.
- Get a good night's sleep the night before. Make sure to eat before your deposition, as the length of depositions can vary.
- Arrive early for your deposition so that you have time to get comfortable with your surroundings.
- Relax. You are going to be asked questions about matters you know about. Your deposition is likely to begin with routine matters such as your educational and work history. No one knows the facts of your case better than you do.
- Tell the truth.

- Stay calm. Your spouse's lawyer will be judging your credibility and demeanor.
- Do not argue with the attorneys.
- Listen carefully to the entire question. Do not try to anticipate questions or start thinking about your answer before the attorney has finished asking the question.
- Answer the question directly. If the question calls only for "yes" or "no," provide such an answer.
- Do not volunteer information. If the lawyer wants to elicit more information, he or she will do so in following questions.
- If you do not understand the question clearly, ask that it be repeated or rephrased. Do not try to answer what you *think* was asked.
- Take your time and carefully consider the question before answering. There is no need to hurry.
- If you do not know or cannot remember the answer, say so. That is an adequate answer.
- Do not guess. If your answer is an estimate or approximation, say so. Do not let an attorney pin you down to facts about which you are uncertain. For example, if you cannot remember the number of times an event occurred, say so. If the attorney asks you if it was more than ten times, answer only if you can. If you can provide a range (more than ten but less than twenty) with reasonable certainty, you may do so.
- If an attorney mischaracterizes something you said earlier, say so.
- Speak clearly and loudly enough for everyone to hear you.
- Answer all questions with words, rather than gestures or sounds. "Uh-huh" is difficult for the court reporter to distinguish from "unh-unh" and may result in inaccuracies in the transcript.
- If you need a break at any point in the deposition, you have the right to request one. You can talk to your attorney during such a break.

- Discuss with your lawyer in advance of your deposition whether you should review the transcript of your deposition for its accuracy or whether you should waive your right to review and sign the deposition.

Remember that the purpose of your deposition is to support a good outcome in your case. Completing it will help your case to move forward.

5.18 Are depositions always necessary? Does every witness have to be deposed?

Depositions are less likely to be needed if you and your spouse are reaching agreement on most of the facts in your case and you are moving toward a settlement. They are more likely to be needed in cases where child custody remains in dispute or where there are complex financial issues.

5.19 Will I get a copy of the depositions in my case?

Ask your attorney for copies of the depositions in your case. It will be important for you to carefully review your deposition if your case proceeds to trial.

6

Negotiation, Mediation, and Collaborative Divorce

Although the dissolution of your marriage is a status conferred upon you and your spouse by a court of law, the "nuts and bolts" of your divorce judgment need not be decided by the court. Although it is not always possible to do so, most divorce cases settle by an agreement reached between the spouses, without the need for an actual court trial.

How does this occur? It occurs when an agreed-upon outcome is reached between the parties on all of the disputed issues in the case. The agreement may be reached through any of several different formats: *conventional* or *traditional negotiation, mediation,* or a format called *collaborative divorce practice.* Whichever way your agreement is reached, it allows you and your spouse to resolve your disputed issues without presenting your case to the judge in a trial, on terms you have had a part in negotiating and agreeing upon.

There are many advantages to a negotiated resolution, if such a resolution can be reached. Among these benefits is a known and certain outcome, minimal risk of an appeal, and the possibility of lower legal fees—perhaps significantly lower.

It is often said that people may be more likely to comply with their respective obligations if they are the product of a negotiated resolution, rather than if the resolution is imposed upon them by a court after a contested trial. Additionally, a negotiated resolution can enhance the prospects of parting amicably, and of being able to work together to raise the children jointly. Despite the circumstances which led to the end of your marriage, it might be possible for your divorce to conclude peacefully by a resolution negotiated with the help of any of these tools. As with anything else, there are advantages and disadvantages to each of them. In all cases, however, it is important to remember that any settlement requires your participation and agreement—no one can settle your case unless you agree to the terms of the settlement.

6.1 What is the difference between *conventional negotiation* and *mediation?*

Conventional negotiation, or shall we say, *traditional negotiation* is by far the most commonly used form of dispute resolution short of going to trial. It is the most flexible method of what is called *alternative dispute resolution,* that is, modalities that can resolve a case without the need for a trial. Negotiation techniques can be employed in any number of formats or in a combination of formats.

For instance, letters between counsel, outlining each parties' suggestions for a proposed resolution, are often employed. Sometimes, agreements may be reached through this exchange of correspondence alone; alternatively, the exchanges of correspondence may serve to narrow issues that may be refined and ultimately resolved over the telephone by the attorneys, or in the conference rooms of a law office with the parties.

Sometimes it may be desirable for the parties to schedule a series of meetings with their respective lawyers, jointly, or at least so that everyone is present and available within the same office suite, to discuss and agree upon a process by which information will be exchanged and shared, agreements will be negotiated, and key disputed issues resolved. Any or all of these methods may be used individually or in virtually any combination to reach a negotiated settlement of the disputed issues in your case.

Mediation is a process in which a lawyer, who is trained in mediation, meets with the parties directly or with their attorneys present. The mediator, sometimes called a *neutral,* attempts to facilitate the reaching of an agreement between the parties by discussing their objectives and trying to help them reconcile them with the resources available to them. The mediator cannot, and does not, represent either party; this individual's role is to facilitate the reaching of an agreement through a series of meetings and conversations. Mediation is non-binding and can conclude at any time either of the parties wishes to end it.

Lawyers for the spouses may be present during mediation, although their involvement is usually less direct than in traditional negotiation. You should still be represented by an attorney in your divorce case, as should your spouse. Your attorney's role will be to assist you in evaluating possible outcomes and alternative scenarios being discussed in the mediation. Your attorney can also help assure that the information being relied upon in the mediation sessions is meaningful, accurate, and verifiable—it is backed-up by reliable data. If an agreement is reached, your attorney's role will also involve making sure the language of the agreement document accomplishes what you intended and thought you agreed to, and that it is specific enough to be enforceable by the court if the other party fails to comply with it in the future.

If it is successful in helping the parties reach a settlement, mediation, like traditional negotiation, enjoys the advantages of a negotiated settlement just discussed: a certain outcome with little risk of appeal and the possibility of lower legal fees. Negotiation and mediation essentially involve differing formats for a process of give-and-take, intended to ultimately reach an agreed-upon settlement in your divorce case.

It is certainly possible that neither method will work in a given case or between two particular individuals. Both traditional negotiation and mediation require the existence of full and truthful disclosure of financial information, as well as information which will bear upon the parties' respective financial circumstances in the future such as their educations and their health. In the absence of full and truthful disclosure, it is not likely that a settlement will be reached in most cases. No one wants to accept a deal offered to them in a dark room where one cannot see what is there. Full and truthful disclosure of information illuminates the room so that everyone knows what is there, and allows each party to make an educated decision on each issue, rather than accepting a proposition "on faith."

Mediation may not be appropriate when one of the parties perceives a history of abuse or intimidation in the marriage, or when there is any interpersonal barrier to communication between the parties which could impair the ability of one or both to speak for his or her own interests in joint meetings. Nor is mediation appropriate when the parties do not have a relatively equivalent understanding of their finances, or of the finances of a family business or professional practice upon which the parties rely for their income.

Sometimes, one spouse may desire mediation and the other may not. Although there is not universal agreement on this point, unless both parties agree that their case is an appropriate one for mediation, it probably is not, and the parties should probably rely upon traditional negotiation.

6.2 How are *mediation* and *negotiation* different from a collaborative divorce?

Collaborative divorce, like traditional negotiation or mediation, is another method of resolving a divorce case in which both parties have a strong commitment to settling their disputes and avoiding litigation. Let's call it "capital C" collaborative, because any method of negotiation or mediation may, and often does, involve a degree of collaboration or cooperation, working together to narrow issues and exchange necessary information. However, those who practice "collaborative law" use the term "collaborative" in an almost proprietary way, to define the approach to negotiation for which they advocate.

In a collaborative divorce, the parties each hire a divorce attorney trained in the collaborative law process. What distinguishes this method of dispute resolution from mediation and traditional negotiation is that you, your spouse, and your respective lawyers must enter into a written *collaborative law agreement* at the outset of the case. This agreement provides that the parties and their lawyers will try to negotiate a settlement through a collaborative process with their lawyers and any other advisors; they also agree to work simultaneously in multiple, joint sessions in an attempt to achieve a settlement.

Often, spouses in the collaborative process enlist the support of other professionals, such as a financial advisor or a "divorce coach," or often a therapist, who will attend the sessions to offer support or other guidance. The hallmark of the collaborative law agreement is that in the event a settlement is not achieved and the case must be tried to the court, neither attorney may represent their client any further, and each must conclude their representation. The divorcing couple must choose new attorneys.

Collaborative law practice is presently the least commonly used approach to a negotiated resolution, but there are attorneys trained in collaborative divorce practice throughout the state of Missouri. Although mediation has become a generally accepted format for dispute resolution in cases which are appropriate for it, collaborative divorce remains a somewhat controversial approach within the family law field, and may have as many critics as it has advocates. Nevertheless, collaborative law appears to be here to stay, and one who is interested in it should have a detailed discussion about it with his or her attorney.

6.3   What is involved in the mediation process? What will I have to do and how long will it take?

The mediation process will be explained to you in detail by the mediator at the start of the mediation session. Mediation involves one or more meetings with you, your spouse, and the mediator. In some cases the attorneys will also be present.

Prior to meeting with the you and your spouse in an initial mediation session, the mediator may conduct an individual initial screening session with each of you to assess your ability to communicate with each other and for domestic intimate partner abuse or other forms of intimidation or coercion. After the mediator's initial screening, he or she will decide whether you and your spouse should mediate together, or whether your mediation should take place separately.

The mediator will likely outline ground rules in hopes of assuring you will be treated respectfully and given an opportunity to be heard. Often, you and your spouse will each be given an opportunity to comment what is important to you in the outcome of your divorce.

How long the process of mediation continues depends upon many of the same factors that affect how long your divorce will take. These include how many issues you and your spouse disagree about, the complexity of these issues, the unrestricted availability of critical information, and the willingness of each of you to work toward an agreement.

Your case could settle after just a couple of mediation sessions or it might require a series of meetings. It is common for the mediator to clarify at the close of each session whether the parties are willing to continue with another session.

6.4   Can negotiation or mediation lower the costs of my divorce?

There can be many advantages to reaching a settlement, and the reduction of the cost of preparing for and trying the case is one of them. Certainly, if the case is negotiated or mediated to a resolution well in advance of a trial date, it can substantially lower the cost of your divorce. You may be able to save thousands (perhaps many thousands) of dollars in legal fees and other costs of litigation, such as expert-witness fees and other costs of litigation support.

If your case is not settled by agreement, you will be going to trial. If the issues in your case are many or if they are complex and involve issues such as child custody, spousal support, the valuation of a business or determination of actual cash flow, the attorney fees and other costs of a properly prepared and conducted trial can be tremendous.

It is during the preparation phase for trial that the transactional costs of divorce litigation really escalate; however, it is an unfortunate fact of life that sometimes it is not until the other side (or you) are fully aware of the risks of a trial, after development of all of the evidence, witness testimony and other preparation, that the case can be settled. A resolution closer to trial, or the day of trial, may still have many beneficial aspects for both parties, but at such a late date, it is less likely that saving money on fees and costs will be one of them.

A wise colleague has often said that "it takes two people to make peace, and only one person to make a war." Despite your best intentions and despite what may be the total reasonableness of your objectives in the divorce case, you may still have to have to go to trial if your spouse cannot be reasoned with or has unrealistic expectations. Ask your attorney about the cost of a trial so that you have some idea of these costs when deciding whether to settle an issue or to take it to trial before the judge.

6.5   Are there other benefits to achieving a settlement?

Yes. A divorce resolved by agreement can have these additional benefits:

Recognizing common goals. Negotiation, whether through traditional or conventional means, mediation, or a "collaborative law" approach, allows for brainstorming between the parties and lawyers. Looking at all possible solutions, even the impractical ones, invites creative solutions to common goals. For example, suppose you and your spouse both agree that you need to pay your spouse some amount of equity for the family home you will keep, but you have no cash to make the payment. Together, you might come up with a number of options for accomplishing your goal and select the best one.

Addressing the unique circumstances of your situation. A settlement reached by agreement allows you and your spouse to consider the unique circumstances of your situation in formulating a good outcome. For example, suppose you disagree about the parenting times for the Thanksgiving holiday. The court may order you to alternate the holiday each year, even though you both would have preferred to have your child share the day with each of you.

Creating a safe place for communication. A negotiated settlement gives each party an opportunity to be heard. Perhaps you and your spouse have not yet had an opportunity to share directly your concerns about settlement. For example, you might be worried about how the temporary parenting time arrangement is impacting your children, but have not yet talked to your spouse about it. A mediation session or settlement conference can be a time and place for you and your spouse to communicate your concerns about your children.

Fulfilling your children's needs. You may see that your children would be better served by you and your spouse deciding their future rather than by a judge who does not know, love, and understand your children like the two of you do—and by the way, the judge is the first person who will tell you this. Of all the difficult cases to decide, most judges who hear family law cases find that child custody cases are the most tragic, difficult, and vexing dilemmas they are ever called upon to decide. They weigh heavily upon the judge who is called upon to determine them. Nevertheless, even the most well considered solution offered by the decision of a judge may not be the right decision for your children.

Eliminating the risk and uncertainty of trial. If a judge decides the outcome of your divorce, you give up control over the result. The judge's decision will be the order of the court on all issues. At that point, there's no going back, and your ability to have input and be a part of the resolution is lost. If you and your spouse reach agreement, you have the power to eliminate the risk of an uncertain outcome.

Another uncertainty pertaining to a trial is that of when the case will be over. In most Missouri courts, just because the trial concludes on Wednesday doesn't mean the court's ruling will occur the same day. Having been called upon to decide issues of this import, most judges will take the time to carefully deliberate over the evidence, review and analyze the proposed judgments of the parties, and make a ruling later—perhaps many, many months later. Thereafter, the postjudgment process and a possible appeal may add a year or more to the time the case is pending. Alternatively, a negotiated settlement will be entered as a judgment by the court very close to the time it is presented to the court for approval, often the same day.

Reducing the risk of harm to your children. If your case goes to trial, it is likely that you and your spouse will give testimony that will be upsetting to each other. As the conflict increases, the relationship between you and your spouse inevitably deteriorates. This can be harmful to your children. Contrast this a process of negotiation, in which you open your communication and seek to reach agreement. It is not unusual for the relationship between the parents to improve as they participate in a process with their lawyers and, if necessary, other professionals, to create a productive environment for rebuilding communication and reaching agreements in the best interest of a child.

Having the support of professionals. Using trained professionals, such as lawyers, accountants, and therapists to support you can help you to reach a settlement that you might think is otherwise impossible. These professionals have skills to help you focus on what is most important to you, and shift your attention away from irrelevant facts and from decisions based more upon emotion and anger than on rational analysis, and which have implications for the short term as well as the long term.

If you have confidence in your attorney (and you should, or you should find another one) you should listen to their advice—you're paying for it; you must have thought there was some value to hiring the attorney. The attorney should be someone you rely upon to know the likely range of possible outcomes if your case goes to trial; a thoughtful evaluation of this range of possibilities is critical to your ability to weigh the pros and cons of a negotiated settlement.

Lowering stress. The process of preparing for and going to court is very stressful. Your energy is also going toward caring for your children, looking at your finances, and coping with the emotions of divorce. You might decide that you would be better served by settling your case rather than proceeding to trial.

Achieving closure. When you are going through a divorce, the process can feel as though it is taking an eternity. By reaching agreement, you and your spouse are better able to put the divorce behind you and move forward with your lives.

6.6   Is mediation mandatory?

Mediation is not mandatory as a matter of Missouri law. In some Missouri counties, however, an attempt at mediation may be required at some point in the case. Your attorney will know whether it is required in the county where your case is filed.

6.7   My spouse abused me and I am afraid to participate in mediation. Should I participate anyway?

If you have been a victim of domestic violence by your spouse, it is important that you discuss the appropriateness of mediation with your attorney. Under these circumstances, mediation may not be a safe or appropriate way for you to reach agreement.

Prior to allowing mediation to proceed, any mediator should ask you whether you have been a victim of domestic violence. This is critical for the mediator to both assess your safety and to ensure that the balance of power in the mediation process is maintained.

Talk with your attorney if you have experienced domestic violence or if you feel threatened or intimidated by your spouse in any way. If so, your case may be referred to an approved specialized mediator for parents involved in high conflict situations; alternatively, it may be possible to mediate with you and your spouse in different rooms or during separate sessions. And it just may be that mediation is simply not appropriate for your case.

If you feel threatened or intimidated by your spouse but still want to proceed with mediation, talk to your attorney about him or her attending the mediation sessions with you. Request to have the mediation occur at your lawyer's office, where you feel more comfortable. If you do participate in mediation, insist that your mediator have a good understanding of the dynamics of domestic abuse and how they can impact the mediation process.

6.8   What training and credentials do mediators have?

There is no required certification for divorce mediators in Missouri, and the background and training of mediators varies. Some are attorneys; some come from other backgrounds such as the mental health professions. Ask your attorney for help in finding a qualified mediator who has completed training in mediating family law cases. The availability of mediators also varies, depending upon where you live.

6.9   What types of issues can be negotiated or mediated?

All of the issues in your case can be negotiated and, in appropriate cases, mediated. Determinations of child custody, child support, spousal support, division of property, and all other aspects of your divorce may be negotiated or mediated. However, in advance of any mediation or negotiation session, you should discuss with your lawyer which issues you want to be mediated or negotiated.

Also, you may decide that certain issues are non-negotiable. Discuss this with your attorney in advance of any mediation or negotiation sessions so that he or she can discuss the possible

85

implications of this decision, and develop a strategy to support you in focusing the negotiations on subjects you agree may be negotiated.

6.10 What is the role of my attorney in the mediation process?

The role of your attorney in the mediation process will vary depending upon your situation. Your attorney can assist you in identifying which issues will be discussed in mediation and, if appropriate, which issues are better left to negotiation between the lawyers, or a judge. Your attorney will also be available to answer your questions and to counsel you about the ramifications of any matter being discussed in mediation. Your attorney should be familiar enough with you to monitor your demeanor and attitude. He or she should be aware of your personality and be sensitive to when you are tired, or having difficulty understanding something in mediation and are in need of a break.

Further, if an agreement is reached in mediation, It is important to understand that until the language of the marital settlement agreement and, where relevant, the parenting plan, are correct and enforceable, the settlement should not be submitted to the court for review. Your attorney will be instrumental in assuring that the language of all settlement documents accomplishes what you believe you settled the case for. In essence, your attorney should be available to you for all advice and counsel you need to try to reach a mutually agreed-upon settlement.

In Missouri, divorce settlements are not binding upon the parties until their particular settlement has been approved by the court. The law in Missouri generally requires that before the court can make such a determination, the parties must come to the court "in present agreement" with its terms. This means that no settlement is really binding until the court has confirmed that at the time it is being submitted for approval, both parties desire that it be approved.

In some courts, the parties must appear and participate in a non-contested hearing, during which they are examined by their respective attorneys and confirm to the court that it is their wish that the settlement be approved. In other courts, local rules may allow an appearance "by affidavit." This means that in lieu of a personal appearance in a hearing, the settlement agreement may be submitted to the court for review so long as it is accompanied by signed affidavits of the parties, expressing their understanding of the settlement terms and their wish that the settlement be approved by the court.

6.11   How do I prepare for mediation?

Prior to attending a mediation session with your spouse, discuss with your attorney the issues you intend to mediate. Enlist your attorney's support in identifying your intentions for the mediation, and make a list of the issues important to you. Be forward looking. Giving thought to your desired outcomes while approaching mediation with an open mind and heart. It is the best way to move closer to settlement.

6.12   Do children attend the mediation sessions?

It is difficult to imagine any situation in which a child should be involved in the divorce case or its negotiated or mediated settlement. In almost all cases, your child will not participate in the mediation. However, one could imagine an exception if you have an older child who is sufficiently mature to participate in the process, on issues specific to the child's schedule and custodial arrangements. However, this is *very* uncommon.

If you think your child should participate in some way, talk to your lawyer and your mediator about the potential risks and benefits of including a child in the process.

6.13   I want my attorney to look over the agreements my spouse and I discussed in mediation before I give my final approval. Is this possible?

Yes. Before giving your final approval to any agreements reached in mediation, it is critical that your attorney review the settlement documents first. He or she should then meet with you to discuss your understanding of the settlement and any discrepancies between your understanding and the language of the settlement document. This is necessary to ensure that you understand the terms of the settlement and its implications. Your attorney will also review the agreement for compliance with Missouri law and for enforceability in the event of non-compliance with its terms at some later time.

Written language means different things to different people and has different effects depending upon context. Words in a settlement agreement that appear to make perfect sense to a layperson, may have a significantly different meaning in the legal context. Only one with legal training can make this determination as to whether the language is sufficient to protect your interests and give life to that which you believe you've negotiated. It is critical that your attorney review the agreement to insure you are protected. He or she should amend and correct the document so that these objectives are, indeed, accomplished by its terms.

6.14   Who pays for mediation?

The cost of mediation must be paid for by you or your spouse. Often it is a shared expense. Expect your mediator to address the matter of fees before or at your first session.

6.15   What if negotiation or mediation fail?

If you elected to pursue mediation, and mediation is not successful, you still may be able to settle your case through negotiations between the attorneys, it may even be possible for you and your spouse to agree to preserve agreed-upon elements of a hoped-for settlement that were reached in either negotiation or mediation. Then, you could take only the remaining disputed issues to the judge for trial.

Sometimes this is not possible, because one or the other of the parties believes they made a significant concession to agree upon one settled point, in hopes that another point would be settled favorably and then it turns out it was not. That party may not agree to "piecemeal" the terms of the ultimate settlement, choosing instead to try the case on all issues rather than only the few which were not resolved by agreement. In a particular case, there may be reasons to do either, and you should discuss with your attorney what the advantages and disadvantages are in your particular case.

6.16   What is a *settlement conference?*

A *settlement conference* can be a powerful tool for the resolution of your case. It is a meeting held with you, your spouse, and your respective lawyers with the intention of negotiating the terms of your divorce. In some cases, a professional with important information needed to support the settlement process, such as an accountant, also may participate.

Settlement conferences are most effective when both parties and their attorneys see the potential for a negotiated resolution and have the necessary information to accomplish that goal. They do not have to be conducted as they are in television shows in which all of the participants are seated together in one conference room and drama and/or hilarity ensue, depending upon the genre of the program.

In fact, although the authors will do it this way occasionally, that is the exception and most frequently such conferences can be more effective if the parties and their lawyers are present in the same suite of offices but not necessarily in the same room. This allows privacy for each party and his or her attorney, and the attorneys may negotiate on behalf of the parties, with the parties present and available in the suite, on the remaining disputed points. There is an efficiency and immediacy to this technique which cannot be duplicated by an exchange of correspondence and phone calls—by the time this meeting occurs, key points will at least have been defined and the negotiations are typically on remaining details or on specified points.

In some cases, a series of such conferences can be an effective way to outline a mutually agreeable approach to the entire case:

- Identifying and agreeing upon what the issues in the case will be
- Agreeing upon what information needs to be produced and how
- Determining whether it might be possible to utilize a financial professional jointly rather than having two dueling expert witnesses
- Agreeing upon temporary financial arrangements and temporary custodial schedules

- Deciding upon a process of how to utilize the influence of the judge during the pendency of the case

There is almost no limit to what items may be discussed cooperatively in this way, if the parties wish it so.

6.17 Why should I consider a settlement conference when the attorneys can negotiate through letters and phone calls?

Your participation and input are necessary to a resolution of your case. A settlement conference can eliminate the delays which often occur when negotiation takes place through correspondence and calls between the attorneys. Rather than waiting days or weeks for a response, you can receive a response on a proposal in a matter of minutes.

A settlement conference also enables you and your spouse, if you choose, to use your own words to explain the reasoning behind your requests. You are also able to provide information immediately to expedite the process.

6.18 How do I prepare for my settlement conference?

Being well prepared for the settlement conference can help you make the most of this opportunity to resolve your case without the need to go to trial. Actions you should take include:

- Provide in advance of the conference all necessary information. If your attorney has asked you for a current pay stub, tax return, debt amounts, asset values, or other documentation, make sure it is provided prior to the meeting.
- Discuss your topics of concern with your attorney in advance. Your lawyer can assist you in understanding your rights under the law so that you can have realistic expectations for the outcome of negotiations.
- Bring a positive attitude, a listening ear, and an open mind. Come with the attitude that your case will settle. Be willing to first listen to the opposing party, and then to share your position to encourage your spouse to listen to your position, listen to hers or his first. Resist the urge to interrupt.

Few cases settle without each side demonstrating flexibility and a willingness to compromise. Most cases settle when the parties are able to bring these qualities to the process.

6.19   What will happen at my settlement conference?

Typically the conference will be held at the office of one of the attorneys, with both parties and lawyers present. If there are a number of issues to be discussed, an agenda may be used to keep the focus on relevant topics. From time to time throughout the conference, you and your attorney may meet alone to consult as needed. If additional information is needed to reach agreement, some issues may be set aside for later discussion.

The length of the conference depends upon the number of issues to be resolved, the complexity of the issues, and the willingness of the parties and lawyers to communicate effectively. An effort is made to confirm which issues are resolved and which issues remain disputed. Then, one by one the issues are addressed.

6.20   What is the role of my attorney in the settlement conference?

Your attorney is your advocate during the settlement conference. You can count on him or her to support you throughout the process, to see that important issues are addressed, and to counsel you privately outside of the presence of your spouse and his or her lawyer.

6.21   Why is my lawyer appearing so friendly with my spouse and her lawyer?

The lawyers representing you and your spouse are professionals who engage in negotiations every day. They didn't create the marital discord with which you are presently burdened, but they are being paid to help resolve it. It would be unproductive if these negotiations all had to be unpleasant and adversarial; it is not likely anyone in the room would have the right attitude to encourage the reaching of agreements on the disputed topics. Also, successful negotiations rely upon building trust between the parties working toward common goals and agreement.

As a professional, your lawyer should be respectful and polite toward your spouse and your spouse's lawyer at all times. It would be doubly productive if your spouse's attorney took the same approach with you and your attorney. In this way, the attorneys can help lead the way to promoting and maintaining the civil, respectful, and dignified atmosphere of trust which is necessary to a good outcome for you.

6.22 What happens if my spouse and I settled some but not all of the issues in our divorce?

You and your spouse can agree to maintain the agreements you have reached and let the judge decide those matters which you are unable to resolve.

6.23 If my spouse and I reach an agreement, how long will it take before it can be finalized?

If a settlement is reached through negotiation or mediation, one of the attorneys will put the agreement in writing for approval by you and your spouse. It may take a few days or perhaps weeks to complete all requested revisions and changes to the documents originally drafted. Once the settlement documents are satisfactory to both parties and their lawyers, your agreement is submitted to the judge for approval either during a noncontested hearing, or by affidavit. It is usually finalized immediately or within several business days.

7

Emergency:
When You Fear Your Spouse

Facing an emergency situation in divorce is as unsettling as any event can possibly be. The emergency may involve physical or emotional abuse, financial abuse, harassment, threats to take the children or loss of access to financial assets. You may not be able to concentrate on anything else. You may be paralyzed with anxiety, with no idea how to begin to protect yourself from such disturbing events. When facing an emergency, do your best to focus on what to do in the immediate moment. Set aside your worries about the future for another day. Now it is time to stay in the present moment, let others support you, and start taking action.

7.1 My spouse has deserted me, and I need to get divorced as quickly as possible. What is my first step?

Your first step is to seek legal advice at your earliest opportunity. The earlier you get legal counsel to advise you about your rights, the better. An initial consultation with an experienced family law attorney will answer most of your questions and help you develop an action plan.

7.2 I'm afraid my abusive spouse will try to hurt me and/ or our children if I say I want a divorce. What can I do legally to protect myself and my children?

If you are truly fearful that your spouse will hurt you or your children, you must develop a plan with your safety and that of your children as your highest priority. Financial and other concerns are secondary to your well-being. In addition

93

to meeting with an attorney at your first opportunity, develop a safety plan in the event you and your children need to escape your home. Resources and information are available online and over the phone: two sources of crisis information are the Office on Womens' Health of the U.S. Department of Health and Human Services, www.womenshealth.gov. This office maintains the National Domestic Violence Hotline, (800) 799-SAFE (7233).

The second resource, the Missouri Coalition Against Domestic and Sexual Violence, maintains a website at www. mocadsv.org. The website provides contact information for agencies, shelters, and domestic violence assistance programs throughout the State of Missouri. Your risk of harm from an abusive spouse may increase when you leave. For this reason, all actions must be taken with safety as the first concern.

Often your local domestic violence agency can help with a referral to an attorney experienced in representing people in domestic violence cases. Talk to your lawyer about the concerns for your safety and that of your children. Your lawyer may suggest you obtain an *order of protection* under the *Missouri Adult Abuse Act*. Where appropriate, such orders may be obtained in any county in Missouri from a court without notice to your spouse. Such orders may offer a number of protections, including granting you temporary custody of your children and ordering your spouse to leave the family residence, and have no contact with you.

It is important to understand that just because you are married does not mean you are not entitled to the protection of your local municipal police force or other authorities, such as the Sheriff's Department in your county, in appropriate circumstances. If you find yourself caught in a situation in which you cannot leave, or in which you fear for yourself or your children, contact the police immediately by dialing 911. They are experienced at dealing with domestic disturbance calls and may be able to assist you in securing temporary assistance and shelter.

7.3 I am afraid to meet with a lawyer because I am terrified my spouse will find out and get violent. What should I do?

When you schedule the appointment, let the firm know your situation and instruct the law office not to place any calls to you that you think your spouse might discover. If possible, pay for your consultation in cash.

Consultations with your attorney are confidential. Your lawyer has an ethical duty not to disclose your meeting with anyone outside of the law firm. Let your attorney know your concerns so that extra precautions can be taken by the law office in handling your file.

7.4 I want to give my attorney all the information needed so my children and I are safe from my spouse. What does this include?

Provide your attorney with complete information about the history, background, and nature of the abuse you have experienced, including any physical proof of the abuse, including:

- The types of abuse (for example, physical, sexual, verbal, financial, mental, emotional)
- The dates, time frames, or occasions
- The locations
- Whether you were ever treated medically
- Any police reports made
- E-mails, letters, notes, or journal entries
- Any photographs taken
- Any witnesses to the abuse or evidence of the abuse
- Any statements made by your spouse admitting the abuse
- Alcohol or drug abuse
- The presence of guns or other weapons

The better the information you provide to your lawyer, the easier it will be for him or her to make a strong case for the protection of you and your children.

7.5   I'm not ready to hire a lawyer for a divorce, but I am afraid my spouse is going to get violent with my children and me in the meantime. What can I do?

It is possible to seek a protection order from the court without an attorney, and independent of whether you seek a divorce. It is possible for the judge to order your spouse out of your home, granting you custody of your children for up to one year, your spouse can be ordered to stay away from you.

7.6   My spouse has never been violent, but I know she is going to be really angry and upset when the divorce papers are served. Do I need a protection order?

The facts of your case may not warrant an order of protection. However, if you are still concerned about your spouse's behavior, ask your attorney about other ways to protect yourself in the event of a divorce filing which you believe will provoke an angry response from your spouse.

7.7   My spouse has been harassing me since I filed for divorce. What can I do?

In Missouri, episodes of physical abuse, emotional abuse, harassment, and stalking may all justify the entry of an order of protection. Talk with your lawyer about whether you should seek the court's protection from your spouse.

7.8   I'm afraid my spouse is going to take all of the money out of the bank accounts and leave me with nothing. What can I do?

One form of abuse can be financial. Occasionally, an angry or controlling spouse may assert control by closing bank accounts or cancelling credit cards with the intention of blocking your access to money. Talk to your attorney immediately. If you are worried about your spouse emptying financial accounts or selling marital assets, it may be critical that you take immediate action. Your attorney can advise you on your right to take possession of certain assets in order to protect them from being hidden or spent by your spouse.

Ask your lawyer about seeking a *temporary restraining order (TRO)*. This order forbids your spouse from transferring, concealing, encumbering or otherwise disposing of marital property until further court order. Such an order is intended to prevent assets from "disappearing" before a final division of the property from your marriage is complete. If this is a concern, talk to your lawyer about the benefits of obtaining a temporary restraining order as to property prior to giving your spouse notice that you are filing for divorce.

Some counties within the state have local rules which provide for the automatic entry of such a restraining order upon filing. For example, in St. Louis County, *Local Rule 68.3.2* states that neither party shall harass or abuse or disturb the peace of the other upon filing for divorce. It also states that a spouse may not cancel utilities, nor transfer, encumber, or conceal assets until further court order. This rule may be enforced by the court.

Also, it is important to remember that even if assets are disposed of, the court may still treat the disposal or concealment of such assets as "dissipation" and, if proven, the court may order the offending party to "make the marital estate whole." Your lawyer can discuss this concept with you.

7.9 My spouse says that I am crazy, that I am a liar, and that no judge will ever believe me if I tell the truth about the abusive behavior. What can I do if I don't have any proof?

Remember that most domestic violence is not witnessed by third parties. Often there is little physical evidence; that doesn't mean it doesn't exist. Even without physical evidence, a judge can enter orders to protect you and your children if you give truthful testimony about your abuse which the judge finds believable. Your own testimony about the abuse you experienced is evidence.

It is very common for persons who abuse others to claim that their victims are liars and to make statements intended to discourage disclosure of the abuse. This is another form of controlling and abusive behavior.

Your attorney's skills and experience will support you to give effective testimony in the courtroom to establish your case. Let your lawyer know your concerns so that a strong case can be presented to the judge based upon your persuasive statements of the truth of your experience.

7.10 My spouse told me that if I ever file for divorce, I'll never see my child again. Should I be worried about my child being abducted?

Your fear that your spouse will abduct your child is a common one. It can be helpful to look at some of the factors that appear to increase the risk that your child will be removed from the state by the other parent.

Talk to your lawyer to assess the risks in your particular case. Together you can determine whether statements by your spouse are threats intended to control or intimidate you or whether legal action is needed to protect your child.

7.11 What legal steps can be taken to prevent my spouse from removing our child from the state?

If you are concerned about your child being removed from the state, ask your lawyer whether any of these options might be available in your case:

- A court order giving you immediate custody until a temporary custody hearing can be held
- A court order directing your spouse to turn over passports for the child and your spouse to the court
- The posting of a bond prior to your spouse exercising parenting time
- Supervised visitation

Both state and federal laws are designed to provide protection from the removal of children from one state to another when a custody matter is brought and to protect children from kidnapping. The *Uniform Child Custody Jurisdiction Enforcement Act (UCCJEA)* was passed to encourage the custody of children to be decided in the state where they have been living most recently and where they have the most ties. The *Parental Kidnapping Prevention Act (PKPA)* makes it a federal crime for a parent to kidnap a child in violation of a valid custody order. Also, in Missouri, parental kidnapping is a crime under state law.

If you are concerned about your child being abducted, talk with your lawyer about all options available to you for your child's protection.

7.12   How quickly can I get a divorce in Missouri?

There are a number of time requirements for getting a divorce in Missouri. Either you or your spouse must have been a resident of Missouri for more than ninety days immediately prior to the filing of the petition for the divorce with the court. After you file your divorce, your spouse must be given notice of the divorce.

A thirty-day waiting period is required for every Missouri divorce. This period begins on the filing date of the petition. The soonest your case can be resolved is after the thirty-day waiting period has expired, although most cases do not get resolved this quickly. The length of time your case remains pending depends in large part upon the extent to which you and your spouse reach agreement on the issues in your case, and upon the complexity of the issues presented by your case.

Your divorce becomes final for most purposes thirty days after the judge signs your divorce decree.

7.13   I really need a divorce quickly. Will the divorce I get in another country be valid in Missouri?

If you are physically present in Missouri and intend to remain in Missouri indefinitely, Missouri is your state of residence. It is not likely Missouri will recognize a divorce obtained in a country in which you do not reside and which does not provide for due process of law substantially similar to that in the United States. Such a divorce judgment would likely be deemed to have been fraudulently obtained. Nevertheless, the only way to know for sure is to consult your attorney, who may have to conduct some legal research regarding the country you are considering.

7.14   If either my spouse or I file for divorce, will I be ordered out of my home? Who decides who gets to live in the house while we go through the divorce?

If you and your spouse cannot reach an agreement regarding which of you will leave the residence during the divorce, the judge may be asked to decide whether one of you should be granted exclusive possession of the home until the case is concluded, or alternatively, you and your spouse may certainly continue to live in the residence during the pendency of your case. This is not ideal, but it is a practical and economic reality for many. Missouri law allows the court to grant exclusive residence of the home to a party in a divorce case when there is potential for emotional harm; but as a practical matter, most judges don't like to remove a party from his or her own home.

Abusive behavior may be one basis for seeking temporary possession of the home according to an order of protection. If staying in the home is important to you, talk to your attorney about your reasons so that a strong case can be made for you at the temporary hearing. It is important to note here that sometimes people who would otherwise move out during the divorce, choose not to because they fear they will be giving up rights to the home or to child custody. This is not true, but you should discuss the matter with your attorney. Perhaps after a satisfactory temporary custody agreement is reached, one of the parties will feel comfortable leaving the residence while the divorce is under way.

A wise lawyer who specializes (as a guardian *ad litem*) in representing children in divorce cases once heard two parents arguing over who would leave the residence. The guardian *ad litem* told them, "Children needed two homes where the sun shines, and not a single home with a black cloud over it all the time." This is a valid point.

7.15 My spouse isn't really a threat and doesn't worry me; however, a friend of mine suggested I file for an order of protection to gain a strategic advantage in my divorce. Should I?

Absolutely not! Your friend has given you a terrible piece of advice. You will be filing pleadings under oath, having sworn them to be truthful. Do not file a fraudulent pleading with the court! It's wrong, and it's against the law. Also, it is true that this proceeding is often abused by people acting on advice like your "friend" gave you. However, family court judges are sensitive to this and have long memories. You don't want to make a move based upon a lie, which will cause the judge to disbelieve anything you ever testify to after that. Finally, taking the long view, the abuse of this procedure by those who don't need it could cause a cautious judge in the future to deny the relief to someone who really, truly needs it. Are you prepared to live with that? It's not worth it.

8

Child Custody

Ever since you and your spouse began talking about divorce, the chances are that your children have been your greatest concern. You or your spouse may even have postponed the decision to seek divorce because of concern about the impact on your children. Now that the time has come, you may still have doubts about whether your children will be all right, both during and after the divorce.

It can be difficult not to worry about how the sharing of parenting time with your spouse will affect your children. You may also have fears about being cut out of your child's life as a result of something the court does. However, in the vast majority of cases such a result is far from likely. What is much more likely is that the court will try to fashion a custody plan that maximizes the amount of time the children will spend with both parents, absent a good reason or reasons not to do so.

Child custody cases can be very challenging to everyone involved, including the judge. Most judges prefer not to have to make these decisions, as they recognize that usually it is the parents themselves who are truly the most knowledgeable about the needs of their children, and they understand that the children are the most important parties in the case. Accordingly, it is usually far more favorable to have the decisions on matters pertaining to child custody made between the parties themselves in an agreed-upon arrangement.

The court is not likely to wish to make these decisions in a trial unless it is satisfied that it is truly not possible for the two parents to reach such an agreement. However, and even despite the best efforts of all, it is sometimes necessary that these decisions be made in court after a trial. Either way, with the help of your lawyer, you can make sound decisions regarding the custody arrangement that is in the best interest of your children.

8.1 What types of custody are awarded in Missouri?

Under Missouri law, there are two aspects to a custody determination. These are legal custody and physical custody. *Legal custody* refers to the power to make fundamental decisions regarding your children and their health, education, and religious training; decisions such as which schools they will attend, what religious traditions they will be raised in, who their health care providers are and what procedures will be performed.

Legal custody may be awarded to you, to your spouse, or to both of you jointly. If you have *sole legal custody,* you are the primary and final decision maker for the fundamental decisions regarding your children. *Joint legal custody* means that you and your former spouse will share equally in the fundamental decision making for your child, and that neither of you may make unilateral decisions on these topics. If you and the other parent are unable to reach agreement, most joint legal custody parenting plans incorporate a provision with a method for dispute resolution. If that is unsuccessful, you may have to return to court for the decision to be made.

Joint legal custody presumes the existence of many of these factors, called in the Missouri cases a "commonality of interests:"

- Effective and open communication between the parents concerning the child
- A strong desire on the part of both parents to continue to co-parent together
- A history of active involvement of bother parents in the child's life
- Similar parenting values held by both parents
- A willingness on the part of both parents to place the child's needs before their own

- Both parents' willingness to be flexible and compromising about making decisions concerning the child

Missouri law lists a number of factors for the court's consideration in determining the custody of children; however, joint legal custody is the preference, it is the first option the court is to consider. This means, among other things, that it is more likely than not that joint legal custody will be the result in most cases. Only when a party can demonstrate that no "commonality of interests" exists, may the court deviate from an award of joint legal custody. The parent who is with the children will make the day-to-day decisions regarding their care.

Physical custody refers to the physical location of the children, that is, where they spend their time. Like legal custody, it may be awarded to either parent or to both parents jointly. Joint physical custody is sometimes referred to as "shared" physical custody, but technically Missouri recognizes only "joint" or "sole" physical custody.

Whether called "joint" or "sole" physical custody, it is defined more by the substance of the schedule than by its title. Specific periods of custody or visitation time will always be awarded to each parent, regardless of who has physical custody. Provisions for days of the week, school breaks, summer, holidays, and vacations are typically made in detail. In the event that one of your children will reside with you and another child will reside with the other parent, the arrangement is referred to as *split physical custody.*

8.2   On what basis will the judge award custody?

The judge considers many factors in determining child custody, all of which must ultimately bear upon "the best interest of the child." The gender of a parent is not relevant to the custody determination. The statute indicates that the court should consider "all relevant factors," including:

- The wishes of the parents
- The needs of the child for a frequent, continuing and meaningful relationship with both parents and the ability and willingness of parents to actively perform

their functions as mother and father for the needs of the child

- The interaction and interrelationship of the child with parents, siblings, and any other person who may significantly affect the child's best interest
- Which parent is more likely to allow the child frequent, continuing, and meaningful contact with the other parent
- The child's adjustment to the child's home, school, and community
- The mental and physical health of all individuals involved, including any history of abuse of any individuals involved
- The intention of either parent to relocate the child's residence
- The wishes of a child

This list of factors is non-exclusive, meaning the court may consider any other relevant factors bearing upon the best interest of the child or children in issue in a given case.

The court may consider factors such as the safety, stability, and nurturing found in each home, as well as the emotional relationship between the child and each parent, including the nature of the bond between the parent and child and the feelings shared between the child and each parent.

It is important to understand that Missouri no longer follows what was once called the "tender years" doctrine, which formerly gave a preference for custody of very young children to the mother. The abandonment of this doctrine in the law many years ago reflected the many sociological changes that had occurred in family life and family structure since the earlier part of the 20th century.

However, the holdover in public perception remains strong, since it is not at all uncommon to hear someone ask if the court still "favors the mother" in child custody determinations. The enduring strength of this public perception is probably enhanced by media marketing campaigns of some in our profession who claim to represent the interests of only a particular gender of parent, who have been somehow taken advantage of by the law and judicial system.

However, the child custody statute is very specifically a gender-neutral statute, and the gender of the parents cannot be a consideration for the court. The court may consider your ability and willingness to be cooperative with the other parent, and in sharing and promoting opportunities for the child to have contact with the other parent; absent a really good reason for doing so, the reluctance of one parent to allow the child to see or be with the other parent is a serious problem in determining custody and is likely to be held against the offending parent. The court may examine the extent to which you and the other parent provide for your child's daily needs such as nutrition, health care, hygiene, social activities, and education. The court may also consider the extent to which both you and your spouse have attended to these needs in the past.

The child's preference regarding custody will be considered if the child is of sufficient age of comprehension, regardless of chronological age, and the child's preference is based on sound reasoning. Typically, the younger the child, the less weight the court is likely to attach to this factor in the law. Missouri law does not allow a child to choose the parent with whom he or she will reside. Rather, the court may consider the well-reasoned preferences of a child, at any age. The custody of a child with special needs, for example, may be awarded to the parent who is better able to meet those needs.

The judge may also consider whether you or your spouse has fulfilled the role of primary care provider for meeting the day-to-day needs of your child, or whether in fact both of you have been involved in providing these needs.

Domestic Violence. Domestic violence is an important factor in determining custody, as well as parenting time and protection from abuse during the transfer of your child to the other parent. If domestic violence is a concern in your case, be sure to discuss it in detail with your attorney during the initial consultation so that every measure can be taken to protect the safety of you and your children.

In Missouri, the court may still allow periods of custody to a parent who has committed acts of domestic violence to the other parent; however, before doing so, the court must describe what safeguards should be put in place to protect the victim parent from further acts of abuse, the court must assure

Child Custody

that the bad actor's history of domestic violence is not visited upon the child.

8.3 What's the difference between *visitation* and *temporary custody*?

Historically, time spent with the noncustodial parent was referred to as *visitation*. Today, the term *temporary custody* is used to refer to the time a child spends with either parent. This change in language reflects the intention that children spend time with both parents and have two homes, as opposed to their living with one parent and visiting the other.

8.4 How can I make sure I will get to keep the children during the divorce proceedings?

You cannot ensure that your children will stay with you during the divorce process. However, the best way to provide clarity about the living arrangements and respective parenting time with your children during your divorce is to obtain a temporary order either from the court or through negotiation which is then made into a consent order. Informal agreements between parties which are not turned into court orders cannot always be trusted. Additionally, informal agreements with your spouse lack the ability to be enforced by the court. Thus, even if you and your spouse have agreed to temporary arrangements, talk with your attorney about whether this agreement should be formalized into a court order.

Obtaining a temporary order can be an important protection not only for the custody of your children, but also for other issues such as support, temporary exclusive possession of the marital home, temporary protection from your spouse, or attorney's fees.

If you are considering leaving your home, talk with your attorney before making any significant changes to your living situation.

8.5 How much weight does the child's preference carry?

The preference of your child is only one of many factors a judge may consider in determining custody. The age of your child and his or her ability to express the underlying reason for their preference to live with either parent will determine the amount of weight the judge will give to your child's preference. Although there is no age at which your child's preference determines custody, most judges give more weight to the wishes of an older child.

The reasoning underlying your child's preference is also a factor to consider. Consider the fifteen-year-old girl who wants to live with her mother because "Mom lets me stay out past curfew, I get a bigger allowance, and I don't have to do chores." Greater weight might be given to the preference of an eight-year-old who wants to live with his mother because "she helps me with my homework, reads me bedtime stories, and doesn't call me names like Dad does."

If you see that your child's preference may be a factor in the determination of custody, discuss it with your lawyer so that this consideration is a part of assessing the action to be taken in your case.

8.6 How old do the children have to be before they can speak to the judge about with whom they want to live?

It depends upon the judge. There is no set age at which children are allowed to speak to the judge about their preferences as to custody.

If either you or your spouse wants the judge to listen to what your child has to say, a request is ordinarily made to the judge to have the child speak to the judge in the judge's office (chambers) rather than from the witness stand. Depending upon the judge's decision, the attorneys for you and your spouse may also be present.

It is possible that the judge may also allow the attorneys to question the child. If you have concerns about the other parent learning what your child says to the judge, talk to your lawyer about the possibility of obtaining a directive from the court to keep this information confidential.

Typically the testimony of the child is made "on the record," that is, in the presence of a court reporter. This is so the testimony can be transcribed later in the event of an appeal.

In addition to the age of a child, a judge may consider such facts as the child's maturity and personality in determining whether an interview of the child by the judge will be helpful to the custody decision-making process.

8.7   How can I prove that I was the primary care provider?

One tool to assist you and your attorney in establishing your case as a primary care provider is a chart indicating the care you and your spouse have each provided for your child. The clearer you are about the history of parenting, the better job your attorney can do in presenting your case to the judge.

Look at the activities in the chart to help you review the role of you and your spouse as care providers for your child.

Parental Roles Chart

Activity	Parent 1	Parent 2
Attended prenatal medical visits		
Attended prenatal class		
Took time off work after child was born		
Got up with child for feedings		
Got up with child when sick at night		
Bathed child		
Put child to sleep		
Potty-trained child		
Prepared and fed meals to child		
Helped child learn numbers, letters, colors		
Helped child with practice for sports, dance, music		
Took time off work for child's appointments		
Stayed home from work with sick child		
Took child to doctor visits		
Went to pharmacy for child's medication		
Administered child's medication		
Took child to therapy		
Took child to optometrist		
Took child to dentist		

Parental Roles Chart (Continued)

Activity	Parent 1	Parent 2
Took child to get haircuts		
Bought clothing for child		
Bought school supplies for child		
Transported child to school		
Picked child up after school		
Drove carpool for child's school		
Went to child's school activities		
Helped child with homework and projects		
Attended parent–teacher conferences		
Helped in child's classroom		
Chaperoned child's school trips and activities		
Transported child to day care		
Communicated with day-care providers		
Transported child from child care		
Attended day-care activities		
Signed child up for sports, dance, music		
Bought equipment for sports, dance, music		
Transported child to sports, dance, music		
Attended child's sports, dance, music practices		
Attended child's sports, dance, music recitals		
Coached child's sports		
Transported child from sports, dance, music		
Know child's friends and friends' families		
Took child to religious education		
Obtained information and training about special needs of child		
Comforted child during times of emotional upset		

8.8   Must I let my spouse see the children before we are actually divorced?

Unless your children are at risk of harm from your spouse, your children should maintain regular contact with the other parent.

It is important for children to experience the presence of both parents in their lives, regardless of the separation of the parents. Even if there is no temporary order for parenting time, cooperate with your spouse in making reasonable arrangements for time with your children.

When safety is not an issue, if you deny contact with the other parent prior to trial, your judge is likely to question whether you have the best interest of your child at heart. Talk to your spouse or your lawyer about what parenting time schedule would be best for your children on a temporary basis.

8.9   I am seeing a therapist. Will that hurt my chances of getting a reasonable custody award?

Your well-being is important to your ability to be the best parent you can be. It is not uncommon for individuals who are otherwise very capable parents to benefit from the assistance of a therapist, or to be under the care of a physician or psychiatrist for treatment of a mental health condition. Since the statutes provides that the physical and mental health of the parents is relevant to the court's determination on child custody, it sometimes happens that the issue of mental health is raised by a party in a divorce case. However, unless a parent has a very serious mental illness that is not controlled through medication, psychotherapy, or other form of treatment, or unless the parent has a serious personality disorder that is harmful to the emotional development of the children, it is unlikely to be an enduring issue in the case.

Discuss with your lawyer the implications of your being treated by a therapist or other mental health professional. It may be that the condition for which you are being treated in no way affects your child or your ability to be a loving and supportive parent.

Sometimes, one's health records are sought when the mental health of a parent is put in issue in a given case. If that occurs, it is possible that your mental health records may be sought by the other party. If this is a matter of concern for you, ask your attorney to contact your therapist to alert him or her regarding how to respond to a request for your mental health records.

Except for certain specific circumstances, such as where there are allegations of child abuse, your medical and psychological records are confidential. You have the right in most circumstances to prevent them from being given to your spouse's attorney; however, if your mental health is in issue and you assert the medical privilege or therapist-patient privilege, your spouse may have the right to request an independent mental examination.

This is a highly specialized concern and not really one that can be addressed in a broad brush-strokes in a book such as this one. Suffice it to say that you should discuss this topic with your attorney and develop a strategy for how this will be handled under the facts of your particular case.

8.10 I am taking prescription medication to treat my depression; will this hurt my chances of getting a reasonable custody award?

Typically not, but the severity of your mental health condition and its impact on the growth and development of your children may become an issue in the case. Of course feelings of depression and anxiety may be situational and temporary; this is not uncommon during a divorce. If you have any mental health concerns, seek help from a professional. Following through with the recommendations made by your health care provider will likely be favorably considered by the court. As described in question 8.09 above, it is sometimes the case that your mental health records will become relevant to the case.

8.11 Will my children be present if we go to court?

In most instances, no. The court makes every effort to protect minor children from the conflict of their parents. For this reason, most judges will not allow children to be present in the courtroom to hear the testimony of other witnesses.

Although the risk that your spouse may share information with your child cannot be eliminated, it would be highly unusual for a judge to allow a child to hear such testimony in a courtroom.

8.12 I had an affair during the marriage. Will that hurt my chances of getting a reasonable custody award?

Whether infidelity will have any impact on your custody case will depend upon many factors, including:

- Whether the children were exposed to it in any way
- Whether the affair had any impact on the children
- How long ago the episode of infidelity occurred, and how isolated an incident it was
- The quality of the evidence about the infidelity

In determining custody, a court may consider the parent's moral fitness, which includes his or her sexual activity and the emotional development of children. However, these considerations are typically taken into account only if the children were actually exposed to sexual activity or were adversely affected by the exposure to an extramarital relationship—exposure which could adversely affect the emotional development of the children. If you participated in infidelity during your marriage, discuss it with your attorney at the outset so that you can assess its impact, if any, on custody.

8.13 During the months it takes to get a divorce, is it okay to date or will it hurt my chances at custody?

It is never a good idea to begin dating before the end of your divorce case without first consulting your attorney about it. Every case is different, and your attorney can best assess whether and when you can begin to date without a concern that it could adversely affect the outcome of your case. Your dating may be irrelevant if the children are unaware of it.

However, it may not be in the best interest of your children to be exposed to a new relationship when they are still adjusting to the separation of their parents, and this fact may not be lost on the court. If there is no agreement yet on the custody arrangement, it may be best to focus your energy on your children, the litigation, and taking care of yourself.

8.14 Can having a live-in partner hurt my chances of getting custody?

If you are contemplating having your partner live with you, discuss your decision with your attorney first. If you are already living with your partner, let your attorney know right away so that the potential impact on any custody ruling can be assessed.

Your living with someone who is not your spouse may have significant impact on your custody case. However, judges' opinions of the significance of this factor can vary greatly, and it is important to understand that the law gives every judge a great deal of discretion in these cases, and there is no aspect of divorce law in which the trial judge is accorded more discretion than in determinations of child custody. Talk promptly and frankly with your lawyer. It will be important for you to look together at many aspects, including the following:

- How the judge assigned to your case views this situation
- Whether your living arrangement is likely to prompt a custody dispute that would not otherwise arise
- How long have you been separated from the parent
- How long you have been in a relationship with your new partner
- The history and nature of the children's relationship with your partner
- Your future plans with your partner (such as marriage)

Living with a partner may put your custody case at risk—after all, you're not even divorced yet. Think about your children, consider such a decision thoughtfully, and carefully consider the advice of your lawyer.

8.15 I'm gay and came out to my spouse when I filed for divorce. What impact will my sexual orientation have on my case for custody or parenting time?

Sexual orientation of a parent is no longer a relevant consideration in determining child custody in Missouri. Nevertheless, your sexual orientation is not the same thing as your sexual activity. While sexual activity of a parent in the abstract, is usually not a significant factor in determining

Child Custody

custody, it may become an issue if your child is exposed to it in any manner. The court may conclude that such exposure is harmful to the child or bears upon the child's emotional development, and such a conclusion may adversely impact the determination of custody.

8.16   What is considered *abandonment,* and how might it affect the outcome of our custody battle?

Abandonment is rarely an issue in custody litigation unless one parent has been absent from the child's life for an extended period. The intentional absence of a parent's presence, care, protection, and support are all considered.

When abandonment has occurred, a court may consider terminating parental rights, but only if doing so would be in the best interest of the child.

8.17   Can I have witnesses speak on my behalf to try to get custody of my children?

Witnesses are critical in custody cases. At a trial on the issue of child custody, you and the other parent will each have an opportunity to present witnesses who give live testimony, or deposition testimony on your behalf.

Among those you might consider as potential witnesses in your custody case are:

- Family members
- Family friends
- Child-care providers
- Neighbors
- Teachers
- Health care providers

In considering which witnesses would best support your case, your attorney may consider the following:

- What has been this witness's opportunity to observe you or the other parent, especially with your child?
- How frequently? How recently?
- How long has the witness known you or the other parent?

115

- What is the relationship of the witness to the child and the parents?
- How valuable is the knowledge that this witness has?
- Does this witness have knowledge different from that of other witnesses?
- Is the witness available and willing to testify?
- Is the witness clear in conveying information?
- Is the witness credible, that is, will the judge believe this witness?
- Does the witness have any biases or prejudices that could impact the testimony?

You and your attorney can work together to determine which witnesses will best support your case. Support your attorney by providing a list of potential witnesses together with your opinion regarding the answers to the above questions.

Give your attorney the phone numbers, addresses, and workplaces of each of your potential witnesses, and if your attorney will be contacting them, let them know they may expect to hear from your attorney or someone in your attorney's office, so that they know they have your permission to speak to your attorney and answer their questions.

This information can be critical to the role that the attorney has in interviewing the witnesses, contacting them regarding testifying, and issuing subpoenas to compel their court attendance if needed. When parents give conflicting testimony during a custody trial, the testimony of other witnesses can be a significant key to presenting a persuasive case on your behalf.

8.18   Will my attorney want to speak with my children?

In most cases your attorney won't ask to speak with your children. An exception might be where custody is disputed or where either parent has made allegations of abuse or neglect, in which case Missouri law requires the appointment of an attorney as guardian *ad litem,* for the reasons set out in question 8.19.

If your attorney asks to meet with your child, provide some background information about your child first. Let your attorney know your child's personality, some of his or her interests, and any topics that might upset your child. This background will help the attorney exercise the care essential anytime a professional questions a child.

If you are concerned that going to your attorney's office for an interview will cause undue anxiety for your child, ask your attorney whether the interview can take place in a setting which would be more comfortable for your child. This might be a public place or your home.

8.19 What is a guardian *ad litem?* Why is one appointed?

As mentioned earlier, a guardian *ad litem* is an individual who is appointed by the court to represent the best interest of the child. The guardian *ad litem* (sometimes referred to as the GAL), is typically an attorney and is directed by the judge to represent the interests of the child to the court. In essence, the role of the GAL is to serve as the child's lawyer; however, under Missouri law, the GAL's highest duty is to the appointing court, and not the child.

The GAL has the responsibility to represent and advocate for the child's best interest in the proceeding; it is likely that you will be asked to meet with the GAL in order for the GAL to perform his or her own due diligence on behalf of the children. Different guardians *ad litem* have different approaches; some are very hands-off, some very hands-on, and many are in between. Your lawyer probably knows the GAL from other cases and will be in the best position to help you work with the GAL in a constructive way, with the children being the ultimate beneficiaries.

8.20 What is a *child custody evaluator?* Why is one appointed?

If custody is disputed, the court may order a *child custody evaluator* to perform a custody evaluation. The child custody expert's job is to examine the circumstances and the mental health of the parties and how they relate to each other, and to make recommendations to the court concerning custody and parenting time. The child custody evaluator will typically conduct a complete evaluation of the parties, conduct psychological testing, interview the parents and the child, interview collateral witnesses, and evaluate the interaction between the child and both parents.

The expert is also authorized to review and receive information, records, and reports concerning all parties involved, including the mental health records of the parties. The expert will then submit a report to the court with his or her recommendations.

8.21 How might photographs or a video of my child help my custody case?

Sometimes, photographs or videos depicting your child's day-to-day life can help the judge learn more about your child's needs. It can demonstrate how your child interacts with you, siblings, and other important people in your family's life. The photographs or videos can portray your child's room, home, and neighborhood, as well as show your child participating in activities.

Talk to your lawyer about whether photographs or a video would be helpful in your case. Although photographs are more commonly used and are typically sufficient evidence, ask your lawyer if he or she recommends making a video, and if so, what scenes to include, the length of the video, keeping the original tapes, and the editing process.

8.22 Why might I not be awarded sole physical custody?

In determining physical custody and parenting arrangements, the court considers the best interest of the minor child, which include, but are not limited to the following considerations:

- The relationship of the minor child to each parent prior to the commencement of the action or temporary hearing, as well as to their siblings
- The desires and wishes of the minor child, if of an age of comprehension but regardless of chronological age, when such desires and wishes are based on sound reasoning
- The general health, welfare, and social behavior of the minor child

- Credible evidence of abuse inflicted on any family or household member
- You may not be awarded sole physical custody if the judge determines that although you are fit to be awarded custody, it is in your child's best interest that custody be awarded to the other parent. A decision by the judge that your spouse should have sole physical custody does not require a conclusion that you are an unfit parent. Even if the judge determines that you and your spouse are both fit to have custody, he or she may nevertheless decide that it is in the best interest of your child that only one of you be awarded physical custody.

Additionally, you may be denied sole physical custody if the judge determines that you are not fit to be a custodial parent.

8.23   What does it mean to be an *unfit parent?*

Parental unfitness means that you have a personal deficiency or incapacity which will likely prevent you from performing essential parental obligations and is likely to result in a detriment to your child's well-being.

Determinations of your fitness to be a custodial parent will largely depend upon the facts of your case. Reasons why a parent might be found to be unfit include a history of physical abuse, alcohol or drug abuse, or mental health problems which affect the ability to parent.

8.24   Does joint physical custody always mean equal time at each parent's house?

No. Joint physical custody means that each parent has significant blocks of custodial time with the child for substantial lengths of time. However, joint physical custody does not necessarily require that each parent have equal amounts of parenting time.

8.25   If I am awarded joint physical custody, what are some examples of how the parenting might be shared?

In joint physical custody arrangements, many parents follow a 2-2-3 schedule, or a variation in which one parent has

119

the child for two weekdays, the other parent has the child for the following two weekdays, and then the child goes back to the first parent for a three day weekend. Below is an example parenting chart to demonstrate the 2-2-3 schedule.

2-2-3 Parent Schedule

	Monday	Tuesday	Wednesday	Thursday	Friday	Saturday	Sunday
Week 1	Mother at 8:00 A.M.	Mother	Father beginning at 5:00 P.M.	Father	Mother beginning at 5:00 P.M.	Mother	Mother
Week 2	Father at 8:00 A.M.	Father	Mother beginning at 5:00 P.M.	Mother	Father beginning at 5:00 P.M.	Father	Father

Some parents prefer to have a one week on, one week off parenting schedule. However, this can be problematic when the children are particularly young, because the research seems to indicate that children are bonding with both parents into age 7 or 8, and frequency of contact, rather than duration, is very important to this. A week-to-week schedule keeps the children from the other parent for an extended period each week. There are many resources available for fashioning temporary custody schedules based on the childrens' ages and developmental levels. Ask your attorney where such resources might be located.

8.26 How is *legal custody* decided?

The parent who is awarded *legal custody* has the responsibility and authority to make all fundamental decisions regarding the child's welfare. Examples of fundamental decisions, include, but are not limited to issues such as religion, education, and non-emergency medical treatment. You can be awarded either sole or joint legal custody.

If you are awarded sole legal custody, you have the sole authority to make fundamental decisions for your child, such as what school your child will attend, who your child's treating physician will be, and whether your child should undergo elective treatments or surgeries. However, even if you are awarded sole legal custody, you may still be ordered to confer with the other spouse about these issues, and your spouse still has the authority and responsibility to make the day-to-day decisions for your child when he or she is in your spouse's care.

If you are awarded joint legal custody, you and your spouse will share the decision-making authority. This necessitates that you and your spouse are able to communicate and agree upon fundamental decisions regarding your children. You and your spouse might be good candidates for joint legal custody if you share a mutual respect for each other, you are able to communicate effectively, and you are able to cooperate and work together in a co-parenting relationship.

If you share joint legal custody and are unable to reach agreement on a major decision, such as a child's school or child-care provider, you and your former spouse may be required to resolve your dispute through some dispute-resolution mechanism incorporated into your parenting plan, or to return to court for a determination of the issue. This can lead to delays in decision-making for matters important to your child, increased conflict, and legal fees.

However, although joint legal custody is the presumptively appropriate order under Missouri law, it is possible the court will not award joint legal custody. The court may do this if you and your spouse disagree about the fundamental decisions regarding your child's welfare or if you are unable to be consistent and support each other in decisions regarding your children. Additionally, if domestic violence has been present in the marriage, it is unlikely that the court will award joint legal custody.

8.27 If my spouse is awarded physical custody of my child, how much time will our child spend with me?

Parenting time schedules for noncustodial parents vary from case to case. However, historically, the most common schedule for non-custodial parents was alternating weekends and one evening during the week, overnight. Additionally, holidays are typically alternated between the parents and Mother's Day and Father's Day are spent with the appropriate parent. Holiday parenting time usually supersedes the regular weekly schedule for parenting time.

121

As in the determination of custody, the best interest of the child are what a court considers in determining the parenting time schedule. Among the factors which can impact a parenting time schedule are the past history of parenting time, the age and needs of the child, and the parents' work schedules.

If you and your spouse are willing to reach your own agreement about the parenting time schedule, you are likely to be more satisfied with it than with one imposed by a judge. Because the two of you know your child's needs, your family traditions, and your personal preferences, you can design a plan uniquely suited to your child's best interest.

If you and your spouse are unable to reach an agreement on a parenting time schedule, either on your own or with the assistance of your lawyers or a mediator, the judge will decide the schedule.

8.28   What does it mean to have *split custody?*

As mentioned earlier, *split custody* refers to a custodial arrangement whereby each parent has sole physical custody of one or more of the children. Courts generally disfavor split custody because it separates the children from each other. However, in families with a disabled child, or a child who is in need of additional health services, or where there is a significant disparity in the ages of the children, the use of split custody can provide for more attention and care focused upon the child in need, or appropriate parental supervision based upon the age of the child.

8.29   What is a *parenting plan?*

A *parenting plan* is a document required by Missouri law which details how you and your spouse will be parenting your child after the divorce. Among the issues addressed in a parenting plan are:

- Custody, both legal and physical
- Parenting time, including specific times for:
    - Regular school year
    - Holidays
    - Birthdays
    - Mother's Day and Father's Day

- ◆ Summer
- ◆ School breaks
- Phone access to the child
- Communication regarding the child
- Access to records regarding the child
- Notice regarding parenting time
- Attendance at the child's activities
- Decision-making regarding the child
- Exchange of information such as addresses, phone numbers, and care providers

Ironically, when parents work well together, they shouldn't need a parenting plan; when parents do need a parenting plan, it may seem they are poor candidates for joint custody. In any event, parenting plans are required by law. There are many specimen plans available to review.

The *Missouri Rules of Court* includes a specimen plan approved by the Missouri Supreme Court; many counties have their own preferred specimen plans, all of which may be customized in any number of respects to accommodate the agreements of the parties or the court's orders. Detailed parenting plans are good for children and parents. They increase clarity for the parents, provide security for the child in knowing what to expect. Having plans reduces conflict, and lowers the risk of needing to return to court for a modification of your divorce decree.

8.30 I don't think it's safe for my children to have any contact with my spouse. How can I prove this to the judge?

Keeping your children safe is so important that this discussion with your attorney requires immediate attention. Talk with your attorney about a plan for the protection of you and your children. Options might include a protection order, supervised visitation, or certain restrictions on your spouse's parenting time, such as no overnight visitation. However, it is rare for the court to enter a no-contact order with respect to children, and the court is likely to do so only when convinced that the children are at risk of harm or neglect when with the other parent.

Make sure your attorney understands the basis for your concerns for the welfare of your children. Suspicions and generalities are not going to carry the day here; specific concerns based upon actual events are what is required to convince the court to limit access to the children by their other parent. Give your attorney a complete history of the facts upon which you base your belief that your children are not safe with the other parent. Although the most recent facts are often the most relevant, it is important that your attorney have a clear picture of the background as well.

Your attorney also needs information about your spouse, such as whether your spouse is or has been:

- Using alcohol or drugs
- Treated for alcohol or drug use
- Arrested, charged, or convicted of crimes of violence
- In possession of firearms
- Subject to a protection order for harassment or violence

8.31 How can I get my spouse's parenting time to be supervised?

Supervised visitation is visitation which takes place in the presence of a responsible adult appointed by the court for the protection of the child. Under Missouri law, a parent's time may be ordered to be supervised under a wide variety of circumstances in which abuse, domestic violence, or any other behavior harmful to the physical or emotional development of the child is present.

Supervised visitation may also be ordered when the parent whose visitation is to be supervised was ever found guilty of, or pled guilty to, any number of criminal acts in which a child was the victim. If you are concerned about the safety of your children when they are with your spouse, talk to your lawyer. It may be that a protection order is warranted to terminate or limit contact with your children. Alternatively, it is possible to ask the judge to consider certain court orders intended to better protect your children.

Ask your attorney whether, under the facts of your case, the judge would consider any of the following court orders:

- Supervised visits
- Exchanges of the children in a public place
- Parenting class for the other parent
- Anger management or other rehabilitative program for the other parent
- A prohibition against drinking by the other parent when with the children
- A random testing regimen for alcohol or drug usage, supervised by the guardian *ad litem* or another responsible individual appointed with ongoing responsibility to monitor these circumstances

Judges have differing approaches to cases where children are at risk, and they have a great deal of discretion under the law to fashion orders that will protect the children. Recognize that there are also often practical considerations, such as cost or the availability of people to supervise visits.

8.32 My spouse keeps saying she'll get custody because there were no witnesses to her abuse and I can't prove it. Is she right?

No. Most domestic violence is not witnessed by others, and judges know this.

If you have been a victim of abusive behavior by your spouse, or if you have witnessed your children as victims, your testimony is likely to be the most compelling evidence.

Be sure to tell your attorney about anyone who may have either seen your spouse's behavior or spoken to you or your children right after an abusive incident. They may be important witnesses in your custody case.

8.33 I am concerned about protecting my child from abuse by my spouse. Which types of past abuse by my spouse are important to tell my attorney?

Keeping your child safe is your top priority. So that your attorney can help you protect your child, give him or her a full history of the following:

- Hitting, kicking, pushing, shoving, or slapping your or your child

- Verbal abuse and name-calling and belittling
- Threats to harm you or the child
- Threatened to abduct your child
- Destruction of property
- Torture of pets or harm to them
- Requiring your child to keep secrets

The process of writing down past events may help you to remember other incidents of abuse that you had forgotten; you will never remember all of the incidents in answer to a spontaneous question about them. The better approach may be to maintain a journal or diary of the events, as you remember them. Cumulatively, you may remember things as you get dressed for the day, as you drive to and from work, as you run errands or in other idle moments. Write down each recollection as you remember it, so that it will not be forgotten. Your cumulative journal of incidents may prove very persuasive and compelling, far more than one or two specific spontaneous recollections made in answer to an unexpected question on the witness stand. Be as complete as possible.

8.34   What documents or items should I give my attorney to help prove the history of domestic violence by my spouse?

The following may be useful exhibits if your case goes to court:

- Photographs of injuries
- Photographs of damaged property
- Abusive or threatening notes, letters, or e-mails
- Abusive or threatening voice messages
- Your journal entries about abuse
- Police reports
- Medical records
- Court records
- Criminal and traffic records
- Damaged property, such as torn clothing

Tell your attorney which of these you have or are able to obtain. Ask your lawyer whether others can be acquired through a subpoena or other means.

8.35 I want to talk to my spouse about our child, but all she wants to do is argue. How can I communicate without it always turning into a fight?

Because conflict is high between you and your spouse, consider the following:

- Ask your lawyer to help you obtain a court order for custody and parenting time that is specific and detailed. This lowers the amount of necessary communication between you and your spouse.
- Put as much information in writing as possible
- Consider using e-mail or mail, especially for less urgent communication
- Avoid criticisms of your spouse's parenting
- Avoid telling your spouse how to parent
- Be factual, and business-like
- Acknowledge to your spouse the good parental qualities he or she displays, such as being concerned, attentive, or generous.
- Keep your child out of any conflicts

By focusing on your behavior, conflict with your spouse has the potential to decrease. Additionally, you should speak with your attorney about developing a communication protocol to follow when communication with your spouse.

8.36 What if the child is not returned from custodial time at the agreed upon time? Should I call the police?

Calling the police should be done only as a last resort if you feel that your child is at risk for abuse or neglect, or if you have been advised by your attorney that such a call is warranted. The involvement of law enforcement officials in parental conflict can result in far greater trauma to a child than a late return at the end of a parenting time. Little in ordinary life leaves a greater impression on a child than having the police arrive to speak to their parents; don't do this to your child unless you have a very good reason and the problem cannot be resolved any other way.

The appropriate response to a child not being returned according to a court order depends upon the circumstances. If the problem is a recurring one, talk to your attorney regarding

127

your options. It may be that a change in the schedule would be in the best interest of your child. Regardless of the behavior of the other parent, make every effort to keep your child out of any conflicts between the adults.

8.37 If I have sole custody, may I move to another town or move out of state without the permission of the court?

No. Under existing Missouri law, any parent with custody of a child must obtain the permission of the other parent before relocating to another state, or even up the street or across town or to another Missouri town. In the absence of such permission, it will be up to the court. There is a specific process set forth in the Missouri laws for pursuing relocation. Therefore, discuss your desire to relocate with your attorney so that you are properly advised as to how to proceed. If your former spouse agrees to your move, contact your attorney for preparing and submitting the necessary documents to your former spouse and the court for approval.

In Missouri, the test for relocation is a very broad one: the intended relocation must be made in good faith, and must be in the child's best interest. This means the relocation must be for a legitimate purpose and not for the purpose of interfering with the other parent's relationship with the child. It also means that the intended relocation must serve the best interest of the child (not necessarily the relocating parent). There can be many reasons to relocate.

In the past, the chance to improve a career, a remarriage to someone with a good job or business somewhere else, and the opportunity to send the child to better schools, have formed the bases of a successful attempt to relocate with the permission of the court. Discuss your circumstances with your attorney in order to evaluate your chances of success.

8.38 I am considering moving out of state. What factors will the court consider in either granting or denying my request to remove my child from Missouri?

If you are considering an out-of-state move, talk to your attorney immediately. In order to leave Missouri with your child, you must have a legitimate reason for leaving the state, such as an increased employment opportunity. The move must also be deemed by the court to be in your child's best interest. In determining your child's best interest, the court may consider many factors, including:

- The potential the move holds for increasing your child's quality of life
- The extent to which your income or employment will be enhanced
- The new living conditions and educational advantages in your new state
- The relationship between your child and each parent
- Your child's ties to Missouri.

The court will also consider the impact that the move will have on the contact between your child and the other parent. Even if you have not finalized your plans to leave Missouri, seek advice from your attorney. He or she can help you gather important information that may be needed in your relocation case, and there are very specific time lines required by the relocation laws.

8.39 After the divorce, can my spouse legally take our children out of the state during parenting time? Out of the country?

It depends upon the terms of the court order as specified in your decree.

If you are concerned about your children being out of Missouri with the other parent, you may want some of these decree provisions regarding out-of-state travel with your child:

- Limits on the duration or distance for out-of-state travel with the child
- Notice requirements
- Information on phone numbers
- Information on physical addresses
- E-mail address contact information
- Possession of the child's passport with the court
- Posting of bond by the other parent prior to travel
- Requiring a court order for travel outside of the country

Although judges are not ordinarily concerned about short trips across state lines, you should let your attorney know if you are concerned that your child may be abducted by the other parent so that reasonable safeguards may be put in place.

8.40 If I am not given custody, what rights do I have regarding educational and medical records, and medical treatment for my child?

Regardless of which parent has custody, state law allows both parents to have access to the medical and educational records of their children. Also, most parenting plans allow either parent to make emergency medical decisions.

8.41 If I'm not the primary caregiver, how will I know what's going on at my child's school? What rights to records do I have?

Regardless of your custodial status, you have a right under Missouri law to have access to your child's school records. Develop a relationship with your child's teachers and the school staff. Request to be put on the school's mailing list for all notices. Find out what is necessary for you to do to get copies of important school information and report cards.

Communicate with the other parent to both share and receive information about your child's progress in school. This will enable you to support your child and one another through any challenging periods of your child's education. It also enables you to share a mutual pride in your child's successes.

Regardless of which parent has custody, your child will benefit by your involvement in his or her education through your participation in parent-teacher conferences, attendance at school events, help with school homework, and positive communication with the other parent.

8.42 If my spouse is awarded legal custody, can I still take my child to my place of worship during my parenting time?

Yes. The determination of the child's religious tradition is a fundamental decision that is made by the parent who has legal custody. However, a noncustodial parent retains the authority to make day-to-day decisions for the child while he or she is in their care. This usually means that a noncustodial parent can still take their child to their own place of worship and participate in religious activities during their custodial time.

8.43 What if my child does not want to go the other parent for parenting time? Can my former spouse force the child to go?

If your child is resisting going with the other parent, it can first be helpful to determine the underlying reason. Consider these questions:

- What is your child's stated reason for not wanting to go?
- Does your child appear afraid, anxious, or sad?
- Do you have any concerns regarding your child's safety while with the other parent?
- Have your prepared your child for being with the other parent, speaking about the experience with enthusiasm and encouragement?
- Is it possible your child is perceiving your anxiety about the situation and is consequently having the same reaction?
- Have you provided support for your child's transition to the other home, such as completing fun activities in your home well in advance of the other parent's starting time for parenting?
- Have you spoken to the other parent about your child's behavior?
- Can you provide anything that will make your child's time with the other parent more comfortable, such as a favorite toy or blanket?
- Have you established clear routines that support your child to be ready to go with the other parent with ease, such as packing a backpack or saying good-bye to a family pet?

The reason for a child's reluctance to go with the other parent may be as simple as being sad about leaving you or as serious as being a victim of abuse in the other parent's home. It is important to look at this closely to determine the best response.

The courts treat compliance with court orders for custodial time very seriously. If one parent believes that the other is intentionally interfering with custodial time or the parent-child relationship, it can result in further litigation and punitive measures. At the same time, you want to know that your child is safe. Talk with your attorney about the best approach in your situation.

8.44   What steps can I take to prevent my spouse from getting the children in the event of my death?

Unless the other parent is not fit to have custody, he or she will have first priority as the guardian of your child in the event of your death. All parents should have a will naming a guardian for their children. In the event you do not intend to name the other parent, talk with your attorney. Seek counsel about how best to provide for your children in the event of your untimely demise.

9

Child Support

Child support is an award of financial assistance from one parent to the other after a divorce judgment. Child support is intended to provide the financial assistance necessary to help cover the cost of common expenses for the children such as food, housing, clothing, and day-to-day living expenses. Whether you will be paying or receiving child support is often the subject of much worry. Will you receive enough support to take care of your children? Will you have enough money to live on after you pay child support? How will you make ends meet?

Most parents want to provide for their children and in Missouri, both parents are legally obligated to contribute to their support. In your divorce case, one of the issues may be how to determine the appropriate amount of this award.

9.1   What determines whether I will receive child support?

Child support, as with almost every other aspect of divorce, is a statutory creature, meaning it is authorized by the Missouri statutes, which describe the factors to be considered by the court in determining whether an award should be made.

These factors include the financial needs and resources of the child; the financial needs and resources of the parents; the standard of living the child would have enjoyed had the marriage not been dissolved; the physical and emotional condition of the child; the child's educational needs; the child's physical and legal custody arrangements, including the amount of time the child spends with each parent; the reasonable expenses associated with the custody or visitation arrangements; and the reasonable work-related child-care expenses of each parent.

The court may consider all of these factors in making its determination on the amount of child support. However, Missouri law also provides that unless there is a good reason to do otherwise, the child support amount calculated on *Missouri Form 14* should be considered the correct amount of child support.

Form 14 is Missouri's version of a set of guidelines for calculating the child support obligation; most states have some method for determining this amount. Form 14 is essentially a work sheet for a calculation based upon the "income shares" model for such charts, meaning the incomes of both parents are considered in the calculation.

One of the rationales for this model is to attempt to provide support at a level the child would have enjoyed had the household remained intact. The methodology of the chart takes into account the "variable" child-related expenses unique to each of the parents' residences, and that there are some child-related expenses which are shared or duplicative. There are numerous such assumptions which form the underpinning of Form 14's child support calculation methodology, and which are described in the notes to Form 14. Form 14 and all assumptions upon which it is based, are available online on the Missouri website: www.courts.mo.gov, under "Court Forms."

9.2 May I obtain temporary child support while waiting for my divorce to be decided?

Yes. Missouri law provides a method for obtaining both spousal and child support while a divorce case is pending. Under the law, a judge has the authority to enter a temporary order for child support. This order ordinarily remains in place until a final judgment is entered.

9.3 How soon can I obtain temporary child support?

Temporary child support is paid sometime after the divorce petition is filed and continues until your final decree of divorce is entered by the court or until your case is dismissed.

If you are in need of temporary child support, discuss the matter with your attorney at your first opportunity; your attorney will be able to explain the process for obtaining temporary support in your county, as well as how long it is likely to take for you to obtain it. Because there are a number of steps to obtaining a temporary child support order, you should not delay in discussing your need for support with your lawyer. Child support will not be ordered for any period prior to the time a request for it was filed with the court.

The following are the common steps in the process:

- You discuss your need for a temporary child support with your lawyer.
- Your lawyer prepares the necessary document requesting the award, and requests a hearing date before the judge.
- On the hearing date, an agreement for temporary support will likely be negotiated; if that does not occur, the matter will be heard by the court.
- The temporary child support order is signed by the judge.
- Your spouse's employer may be notified to begin withholding your support from your spouse's paychecks.
- Your spouse's employer sends the support to the Missouri Family Support Payment Center (FSPC), in Jefferson City, which sends the money on to you.

If your spouse is not voluntarily providing needed financial assistance to you, time is of the essence in obtaining a temporary order for support. This should be one of the first issues you discuss with your lawyer.

9.4 How soon does my spouse have to begin paying support for the children?

Your spouse may begin paying you support voluntarily at any time. A temporary order for support will give you the right to collect the support if your spouse stops paying. Talk to your lawyer about court hearings for temporary support in your county. You may have to wait several weeks, or perhaps even months in some circumstances, before your temporary support hearing can be held. Also, it is possible that the judge will not order child support to start until the first day of the following month. Nevertheless, Missouri law allows for retroactive awards, meaning that the court may award support all the way back to the date the request for temporary support was originally filed with the court.

9.5   How is the amount of child support determined?

The *Missouri Child Support Guidelines* were created by the Missouri Supreme Court in order to prescribe the method by which your child support is calculated. As previously stated, both parents have a duty to contribute to the support of their children in proportion to their respective net incomes. As a result, both your income and the income of your spouse will factor into the child support calculation.

Other factors the court may consider include:

- The additional cost of health insurance for the child, as well as uninsured or court-ordered medical costs
- Regularly paid support for other children
- The cost of work-related child care of the parent receiving support
- The cost of other extraordinary needs of the child
- Whether the amount of time spent overnight with the obligor parent warrants an adjustment to the amount otherwise determined (called the *overnight visitation credit*).

Child support that is higher or lower than what the guidelines provide for may be awarded in certain cases, whenever the judge determines the amount of support otherwise calculated is unjust or inappropriate in the circumstances. This is called a *deviation from Form 14* and the trial judge has the discretion to deviate from the Form 14 amount, based upon the evidence in your case.

You may review the guidelines in greater detail, as well as review examples demonstrating their use, on the Missouri Judiciary website: www.courts.mo.gov, under "Court Forms."

9.6 Will the type of custody arrangement or the amount of parenting time I have impact the amount of child support I receive?

It can. Shared physical custody can lower child support amounts. For this reason, it is essential that you discuss child support with your attorney prior to reaching any agreements with your spouse regarding custody or parenting time.

9.7 Is overtime or bonus compensation considered in the calculation of child support?

Yes, it can be, if your overtime pay or bonuses received are so routinely received as part of your employment that you can actually expect to earn it regularly. The judge may consider your work history, the degree of control you have over your overtime compensation, and the nature of the field in which you work, as well as the impact of your child-care responsibilities on your ability to obtain overtime compensation. There are many factors to be considered by the court and they are described in Comments C and D to "Line 1" of Form 14, available at www.courts.mo.gov in the "Court Forms" section.

9.8 Will other income, such as rental income for example, be considered in determining the child-support obligation, or just salary?

Yes, income from all sources may be considered in determining the amount of child support. Form 14, provides that gross income can include the following:

- Salaries
- Wages
- Commissions
- Dividends
- Severance pay
- Pensions
- Interest
- Trust income
- Annuities
- Partnership distributions
- Social Security benefits

- Retirement benefits
- Workers' compensation benefits
- Unemployment compensation benefits
- Disability insurance benefits
- Social Security disability benefits (SSD) due to a parent's disability
- Veterans' disability benefits and military allowances for subsistence and quarters

In appropriate circumstances the following may be included, in whole or in part, as gross income:

- Overtime compensation
- Bonuses
- Earnings from secondary employment
- Recurring capital gains
- Prizes
- Retained earnings
- Significant employment-related benefits

9.9   My spouse has a college degree but refuses to get a job. Will the court consider this in determining the amount of child support?

Form 14 provides that if a parent is unemployed or found to be underemployed, gross income may be based on *imputed income.* As a result, the earning capacity of your spouse may be considered instead of current income in these circumstances. The court may also consider the work history, education, skills, health, and job opportunities for both parents.

If you believe your spouse is earning substantially less than the income she or he is capable of earning, provide your attorney with details. Ask about making a case for child support based on earning capacity, rather than actual income.

9.10   Will I receive the child support directly from my spouse or from the state?

Missouri law requires that child support be withheld from the income of the payor of child support, unless there is a good reason not to have the support automatically withheld, such as an agreement by the parties otherwise.

If the payor's income is not being withheld by his or her employer, the parent makes child support payments directly to the Missouri Family Support Payment Center (FSPC), a division of the Missouri Department of Social Services, in Jefferson City. The Payment Center then sends the child support to the parent receiving support.

9.11 How will I receive my child support payment?

The Missouri Family Support Payment Center has several methods of disbursing your child support money, including direct deposit into your bank account.

More information may be obtained from the Missouri Family Support Payment Center website at http://dss.mo.gov.

9.12 Is there any reason not to pay or receive payments directly to or from my spouse once the court has entered a child support order?

Yes. Once a child support order is entered by the court, the FSPC maintains a record of all support paid. If the payment is to be made through the Payment Center but instead paid directly, the state's records will show that the payor is behind in paying the child support.

Direct payments of child support can also result in misunderstandings between parents. The payor may have intended the money to pay a child support payment, but the parent receiving the support may have thought it was extra money to help with the child's expenses.

The payment of support through the Payment Center can protect both parents. You should discuss this with your attorney before making a decision.

9.13 If my spouse has income other than from an employer, is it still possible to obtain a court order to withhold my child support from his income?

Yes. Child support can be automatically withheld from most sources of income. These may include unemployment compensation, worker's compensation, retirement plans, and investment income.

9.14 What happens with child support when our children go to other parent's home for summer vacation? Is child support still due?

Typically yes. Whether child support is adjusted during extended parenting time with the noncustodial parent depends upon the court order in your case. For instance, in some circumstances, if a child is with the other parent for thirty consecutive days or more, that parent's obligation to pay support is suspended, or temporarily cancelled, until the regular schedule resumes.

It doesn't sound very complicated, but this can be a hard issue to resolve in some cases, and the facts to which the statute is applied can be murky. Therefore, the matter should be discussed with your attorney. Before your settlement is completed, and your divorce decree is entered by the court, discuss this topic with your lawyer. If you believe the parent paying support will have the child for an extended period, it could mean that special language should be written into the agreement or judgment.

9.15 After the divorce, if I choose to live with my new partner rather than marry, can I still collect child support?

Yes. However, if you are also a recipient of spousal support, your former spouse may have a basis for reducing or possibly even terminating spousal maintenance based upon your cohabitation with another person. Cohabitation will not terminate your former spouse's child-support obligation to you.

9.16 May I still collect child support if I move to another state?

Yes. A move out of state will not impact your right to receive child support under the Missouri judgment. However, the amount of child support could be modified if other circumstances change, such as income or costs for exercising parenting time.

9.17 May I expect to continue to receive child support if I remarry?

Yes. Your child support will continue even if you remarry.

9.18 How long may I expect to receive child support?

Under current Missouri law, child support is ordinarily ordered to be paid until the child becomes emancipated. *Emancipation* occurs when the child dies, marries, joins the military, becomes self-supporting, or reaches the age of eighteen. However, under current Missouri law, if at age eighteen the child remains enrolled in secondary school or enrolls in an institution of higher education or vocational school, support continues until the earlier of the date the child completes or leaves school, or age twenty-one.

Once the child begins to attend post-secondary school, there are specific criteria which must be satisfied in order for the child to remain eligible for the continuation of child support, including minimum credit hours and grades, and disclosure of registration and grades received, to the payor parent upon request.

It is critical to the continuation of child support that you, if you are the recipient of support, and the child for whom the support is awarded, comply strictly with these requirements in order to avoid an interruption (or possibly even a termination) of child support. You should be certain to discuss this with your attorney, and you should check again when the child leaves for college because this language in our statute is often amended and revised.

9.19 Does interest accrue on past-due child support?

Yes, interest accrues on past-due child support. The current statutory interest rate for past-due child support is 1 percent per month (12 percent per year).

9.20 What can I do if my former spouse refuses to pay child support?

If your former spouse is not paying child support, you may take action to enforce the court order either with the help of your lawyer or the assistance of the prosecuting attorney.

Unlike a private attorney, you do not pay for the services of the prosecuting attorney.

Visit the website for the Missouri Department of Social Services at http://dss.mo.gov for further information about child support enforcement.

Many methods of enforcement exist. You may request that your former spouse's state and federal tax refunds be intercepted. You may request that a lien be placed upon certain real estate. You may garnish bank accounts or other assets of the obligor spouse, including retirement assets, to pay past-due child support. You may file a *motion for contempt,* which is a request that the trial court find that the obligor has failed to comply, and seek the payment of a fine or that the payor be incarcerated as an inducement to satisfying the arrearage.

Recreational licenses, driver's licenses, and professional licenses may also be suspended if a parent falls behind in child support payments. You should consult your attorney to discuss which of the options are most likely to be successful in your particular circumstances.

9.21 After the divorce, can my former spouse substitute direct purchases made by him or her for the child, in lieu of actual child support payments?

No. Purchases made for a child by the payor spouse do not relieve the payor spouse from the court-ordered obligation to pay child support, nor are they credited against the amount of the support obligation.

9.22 Are expenses such as child care supposed to be taken out of my child support?

It depends. If the child care is necessary because you are employed during the day, and it is necessary to place your child in day care or another such environment, it can be factored in to the child support calculation. Although they are factored in to the Form 14 calculation, such work-related child care expenses are sometimes determined separately from child support because of the variability of this expense, and it may be that you and your spouse agree upon how the child care expense is to be paid in addition to child support.

9.23 How does providing health insurance for my child affect my child support amount?

If you pay the health insurance premium for your child, the amount you pay will be taken into account on the Form 14 when calculating the presumed correct child support amount. You will receive a credit for your share of the amount you pay per month for your child's health insurance premium.

9.24 Am I required to pay for my child's uninsured medical expenses from the child support I receive?

Your parenting plan will indicate how the cost of unreimbursed medical expenses will be allocated between you and your spouse. One of the assumptions expressed in most parenting plans is that the party receiving child support pays for the first $250.00 per child, per year of uninsured/unreimbursed health care costs, and that the remaining uninsured/unreimbursed health care costs in excess of $250.00 per child, per year, are shared between the parties. However, the terms of the parenting plan in your divorce may differ.

9.25 Am I required to pay for the general, every day expenses for my child with the child support I receive?

Yes, if you are receiving child support under the guidelines, you are responsible for expenses for your child such as housing, clothing, school lunches, and the cost for activities.

However, if you have joint physical custody, you will provide for your child's day-to-day expenses when the child is with you, and the other parent will pay for those expenses when the child is in their care. You will need to coordinate with the other parent for purchases of major expenses.

9.26 Can my spouse be required by the decree to pay for our child's private elementary and high school education?

As a general rule, a Missouri court may only order a party to pay private school expense where the child has a demonstrated special need that cannot be addressed in the public school where the child lives. This means that unless there is agreement between the parents that the child attend a private school, the court cannot impose this payment obligation on a parent. Some parents agree to include a provision in the decree for payment of such tuition because both of them believe it is important for their child. The *Missouri Child Support Guidelines* make no specific provision for private education tuition, although it is the type of expense that could be listed as an "extraordinary" expense of the child in line 6 (e) of Form 14. However, it might be better in your case to deal with payment of private school tuition obligation outside of the Form 14 calculation; a discussion with your attorney about this will help you make the right decision for your case.

If you want your spouse to share this expense for your child, talk it over with your lawyer. Be sure to provide your attorney with information regarding tuition, fees, and other expenses related to private education.

9.27 Can my spouse be required by the decree to contribute financially to our child's college education?

In Missouri, the legal duty of a parent to support a child may include the cost of a college education, depending upon the financial circumstances of the family. In some cases it may be premature to make this determination; unless the children are near college age, no one can really know where the child will want to attend college nor what the financial circumstances of the parents are likely to be.

If your decree includes a provision for payment of college education expenses, be sure it is specific. Language commonly used in Missouri judgments include:

- A definition of what specific expenses are included? For example, tuition, room and board, books, fees, or travel
- A limitation, or cap, on the legal obligation of the payor parent, based upon a standard, "yardstick" school. For example, a common order is that a parent must pay an amount which doesn't exceed fifty percent of the cost for tuition, dormitory room and board, books, based upon the cost to attend the University of Missouri, regardless of which school the child ultimately attends. This allows a court to determine how to allocate the

cost for the child to attend the school of his or her choice. When is the payment due?

- For what period of time does it continue, for example, how many semesters?
- Are there any limits on the type of education that will be paid for?

The greater the clarity in such a provision, the lower the risk is for misunderstanding or conflict years later.

10

Maintenance

Maintenance is an award of support, typically paid monthly, from one former spouse to another after divorce. It is intended to assist the recipient spouse in meeting his or her expenses, in a situation where the incomes of the parties are disparate. Although most people generally understand and accept the concept of the equitable division of marital property, they tend to have a much stronger feelings regarding the concept of spousal maintenance. If your spouse has filed for divorce and is seeking maintenance, you might see it as a double injustice—your marriage is ending and you feel like you have to pay for it, too. If you are seeking spousal maintenance, you might feel hurt and confused that your spouse is resistant to helping support you, even though you may have interrupted your career by agreement with your spouse, to stay home and care for your children.

Understanding Missouri's laws on spousal maintenance can help you move from your emotional reaction to the economic reality of possible outcomes in your case. Uncertainty about the precise amount of maintenance that may be awarded, or the number of years it might be paid, is not unusual. Work closely with your lawyer. Be open to possibilities. Try looking at it from your spouse's perspective. With the guidance of your lawyer, you can make an informed decision on the best strategy to pursue so that you will end up with a maintenance arrangement you can live with after your divorce is over.

10.1 Which gets calculated first, child support or spousal maintenance?

Ordinarily the court calculates spousal maintenance first. One of the inputs into the chart that Missouri courts use to calculate the presumed correct child-support amount (Form 14), is the gross income of each spouse. In order to determine the proper amount of income upon which to determine the child support amount, the Form 14 adds spousal maintenance to the income of the person receiving child support and subtracts it from income of the spouse paying child support.

10.2 What's the difference between *spousal maintenance* and *alimony*?

Although some people still use the terms maintenance and alimony interchangeably, they are not the same thing. Before Missouri implemented the *Dissolution of Marriage Act* in 1974, the state statutes referred to support payments to a former spouse as alimony. *Alimony* was considered an assessment of damages for the payor party's breach of the marital contract. *Maintenance* awards under the *Dissolution of Marriage Act* are periodic payments to a former spouse for the purpose of permitting the recipient spouse to readjust financially until he or she can achieve a reasonable measure of self-sufficiency. Unlike alimony, maintenance is not based on the concept of damage, it is based on the concepts of need and ability to pay.

10.3 How will I know if I am eligible to receive spousal maintenance?

No mathematical formula exists in Missouri to determine one's eligibility for spousal maintenance. The Missouri law that governs spousal maintenance sets forth a two-part test. First, the party seeking spousal maintenance must lack sufficient property to provide for his or her own reasonable needs. Secondly, the individual must either be unable to support himself or herself through appropriate employment, or he or she must be the custodian of a child or children whose condition or circumstances make it appropriate that the parent not be required to seek employment outside the home. After a party passes both prongs of this test, and so long as the other spouse has the ability to pay, the court may award maintenance. The amount will be one the court considers fair after considering the following ten non-exclusive factors:

- The financial resources of the party seeking maintenance, including marital property apportioned to him, and his ability to meet his needs independently, including the extent to which a provision for support of a child living with the party includes a sum for that party as custodian
- The time necessary to acquire sufficient education or training to enable the party seeking maintenance to find appropriate employment
- The comparative earning capacity of each spouse
- The standard of living established during the marriage
- The obligations and assets, including the marital property apportioned to him and the separate property of each party
- The duration of the marriage
- The age, and the physical and emotional condition of the spouse seeking maintenance
- The ability of the spouse from whom maintenance is sought to meet their own needs while meeting those of the spouse seeking maintenance
- The conduct of the parties during the marriage
- Any other relevant factors

Every case for spousal maintenance is unique and stands on its own facts. Talk with your attorney to determine whether you are a candidate for spousal maintenance or whether you may be required to pay it. Providing your lawyer with clear and detailed information about the facts of your marriage and current situation, will allow the attorney to make a spousal maintenance assessment in your case.

10.4 What information should I provide to my attorney if I want the court to award spousal maintenance?

As part of your initial meetings with your attorney, you should discuss whether you or your spouse are candidates for an award of spousal maintenance. Although no attorney will be able to promise any specific results, there is certain information you can provide your attorney that will allow him or her to give you better guidance on your chances of receiving maintenance. This information includes:

- You and your spouse's complete educational backgrounds, including the dates of schooling or training, and degrees earned
- You and your spouse's work histories, including the names of employers, the dates of employment, duties, pay/wages, and the reasons for leaving
- Complete copies of your tax returns for the last several years, including attachments (W-2s, K-1s, 1099s)
- You and your spouse's most recent pay stubs and documentation showing fringe benefits
- Detailed documentation of your monthly living expenses over the course of the last several years
- Detailed documentation relating to anticipated future expenses such as health insurance, housing, taxes, necessary repairs
- A history of any interruptions in your education or career for the benefit of your spouse, including transfers or moves due to your spouse's employment
- A history of any interruptions in your education or career for raising children, including periods during which you worked part-time
- Your health history, including any current diagnoses, treatments, limitations, and medications

The more complete the information is that you provide to your lawyer, the easier it will be for him or her to assess your case.

10.5 My spouse told me that because I had an affair during the marriage, I have no chance to get spousal maintenance even though I quit my job and have cared for our children for many years. Is it true that I have no case?

It is not true, and as stated above, every case stands on its own set of facts. Although court may consider the conduct of the parties during the marriage, including infidelity, the court may consider many other factors as well in determining its award of spousal maintenance. Extramarital relationships do not automatically eliminate awards of spousal maintenance.

10.6   How is the amount of spousal maintenance calculated?

Unlike child support, no precise formula exists for determining the amount of spousal maintenance. A judge will consider all of the statutory factors in arriving at an appropriate amount. Among the most important factors are your reasonable monthly expenses and the funds your spouse has remaining after meeting his or her own reasonable expenses.

Judges have a great deal of discretion in making a decision on spousal maintenance. There are no specific guidelines. Consequently, the outcome of a spousal maintenance award by a judge can be one of the most unpredictable aspects of your divorce.

10.7   My spouse makes a lot more money than she reports on our tax return, but she hides it. How can I prove my spouse's real income to show she can afford to pay spousal maintenance?

Inform your attorney about your concerns. Your lawyer can help you make strategic decisions about how best to determine your spouse's income with greater accuracy. They are likely to include:

- Hiring a CPA or other qualified expert to analyze cash flow
- Issuing subpoenas to financial institutions and tracing the movement of the funds within the accounts
- Examining check registers, bank deposits and ledgers and taking depositions of third parties who have knowledge of income or spending by your spouse
- Issuing subpoenas for records of places where your spouse has made large purchases or received income
- Inquiring into cash-based transactions

Even after employing these strategies, there is no guarantee that you will be able to establish your spouse's actual income as being greater than is shown on tax returns. If you filed joint tax returns, discuss with your lawyer any other implications of erroneous information on those returns.

10.8 I want to be sure the records on the spousal maintenance I pay are accurate, especially for tax purposes. What's the best way to ensure this?

If you are paying child support in addition to spousal support, your spousal maintenance payments should be made to the Missouri Family Support Payment Center in Jefferson City. Spousal maintenance can be automatically withheld from your income, just like child support.

By avoiding direct payments to your former spouse, you both will have accurate records. However, if you do not pay support through the FSPC, you should maintain detailed records of payments made or received. Payments of cash are least desirable since there is no routinely reliable way to prove the payment was made or received. Therefore, it is highly undesirable to pay maintenance in this manner. In any event, the amount you deduct on your tax returns for maintenance paid must equal the amount of maintenance that your spouse reports as income.

10.9 What effect does spousal maintenance have on my taxes?

If you are required to pay spousal maintenance according to a court order, and the order complies with the Internal Revenue Code's criteria, your spousal maintenance payments are tax deductible. Conversely, if you are the recipient of spousal maintenance according to a court order that complies with the Internal Revenue Code's criteria, you must pay income tax on the spousal maintenance you receive. For more information, please see questions 14.4 and 14.5 in chapter 14. Also, ask your attorney.

10.10 What types of payments are considered spousal maintenance?

Payments to a former spouse according to a divorce decree or legal separation are considered spousal maintenance, or alimony, under the tax code. Additionally, payments to others on behalf of, or for the benefit of your spouse, may, under the terms of your divorce decree qualify as alimony for tax purposes. For example, your decree may require your ex-spouse to pay your health insurance premium after the divorce.

If the decree properly characterizes this payment as spousal maintenance, it will be taxable to you and deductible by your ex-spouse. However, it is important to note that you cannot elect to pay for expenses on behalf of your former spouse in lieu of direct payments.

10.11 How is the purpose of spousal maintenance different from the property I receive in the property settlement?

Spousal support and the division of property serve two separate purposes, even though many of the factors for determining them may seem to overlap. The purpose of spousal maintenance is to provide support. In contrast, the purpose of a property division is to distribute the marital assets equitably between you and your spouse.

10.12 My spouse makes a lot more money than I do. Will I be awarded spousal maintenance to make up the difference in our income?

Although the purpose of spousal maintenance is to provide support, spousal maintenance awards are not used as a means to equalize the incomes of a couple. Instead, spousal maintenance awards serve the purpose of allowing a spouse, who is unable to meet his or her own needs during and after the divorce, until he or she becomes economically self-sufficient. If you are able to meet your reasonable needs, based on the income derived from the property you are awarded and your earned income, you are not a candidate for spousal maintenance even if your spouse makes substantially more than you. You should discuss this with your attorney.

10.13 How long can I expect to receive maintenance?

The answer to this question depends largely upon how you resolve your case. If you proceed to trial, the trial judge faces constraints that you and your spouse do not face in establishing an award of maintenance. A divorcing couple can, by agreement, establish an award of maintenance for a specified duration and incorporate provisions in their agreement which are unique to their circumstances. A trial judge does not have the same flexibility. Except under very specific circumstances, the judge must honor Missouri's judicial preference for awards of modifiable spousal maintenance of unlimited duration. Accordingly, the trial judge cannot place limits on spousal maintenance awards based on speculation or insufficient evidence that the parties' circumstances will be different in the future.

A trial court's decision to limit the duration of a maintenance award is warranted only where there is substantial evidence that the spouse requiring maintenance will be able to become self-sufficient within the specified time. Unless the spousal maintenance award falls within this narrow exception, a spousal maintenance award in judgment that results from a trial will likely be both open-ended and modifiable. This means that the original spousal maintenance award will continue (with no fixed ending date) until further order of the court. Either party may file a motion to modify to increase, to decrease, or to terminate maintenance, based upon a substantial and continuing change in circumstances such that the original award should be considered unreasonable.

Alternatively, in a negotiated settlement you and your spouse may agree upon a wide range of options from open-ended modifiable spousal maintenance to a fixed term non-modifiable award. There are fewer constraints for a negotiated agreement. In any event, unless you and your spouse specifically provided otherwise, your spousal maintenance will terminate upon your remarriage or the death of either of you.

10.14 Does remarriage affect my spousal maintenance?

Yes. Unless your divorce decree provides otherwise, under Missouri law, spousal maintenance automatically terminates upon the remarriage of the recipient.

10.15 Does the death of my former spouse affect my maintenance?

Yes. Under Missouri law, unless your decree provides otherwise, spousal maintenance ends upon the death of either party. Although you and your spouse can agree in a negotiated settlement that spousal maintenance will continue past the death of the recipient of spousal maintenance, the court cannot do the same if a case is tried. If you and your spouse do negotiate a settlement that provides for maintenance past the death of the recipient there are tax consequences. Under these circumstances, the maintenance payments cannot be taxable to the recipient or deductible by the payor, even while the recipient is still alive.

10.16 Must I keep paying maintenance if my former spouse is now living with a new "significant other"?

Unless your decree contains a provision which automatically terminates your obligation to pay spousal support in the event of your former spouse's cohabitation, you must continue to pay spousal maintenance. Such a relationship may not be a permanent one and as such, does not give rise the duties of support that a marriage does. Although cohabitation does not itself terminate your spousal maintenance obligation under Missouri law, it may, in some circumstances, provide the basis for a reduction of your spousal maintenance obligation.

There are many factors for the court to consider, and the facts of your particular case will drive this determination. You should contact your attorney with the information you have to discuss whether it is a good idea to attempt to modify the maintenance obligation.

10.17 Can I continue to collect maintenance if I move to a different state?

Yes. Unless your decree of dissolution of marriage contains a specific provision to the contrary, your former spouse's duty to pay the spousal maintenance awarded to you in the decree does not end simply because you move to another state.

10.18 What can I do if my spouse stops paying spousal maintenance?

There are several options available to you in the event that your former spouse stops paying maintenance. In some instances, a demand letter from your attorney will suffice. If your ex-spouse is delinquent in an amount equal to or greater than one month's total support, you can initiate an automatic wage withholding. If you and your spouse settled your divorce and you entered into a separation agreement, you can bring an action against your former spouse for *breach of contract*. Lastly, under most circumstances you have the option of filing a motion to have your former spouse held in *contempt of court* for willfully failing to comply with the terms of the judgment of dissolution of marriage.

In a contempt case, the trial court will issue an order to show cause to be served on your ex-spouse. The order to show cause will set a date and time on which your former spouse must appear before the court and demonstrate good cause for not having made payments. If the court finds your former spouse in contempt, it can order him or her incarcerated or impose daily fines until such time as your ex-spouse pays what is owed. Discuss with your attorney which of these represents your most economical option with the greatest chance of success.

10.19   Can I return to court to modify maintenance?

Unless your divorce decree provides that your spousal maintenance order is nonmodifiable, either party may return to court to attempt to increase, decrease, or terminate spousal maintenance. This process is called *filing a motion to modify* your previous judgment. If you were not awarded maintenance in your original divorce decree, you cannot return to the court at a later date to request that it be awarded to you.

In order for the court to grant a modification of spousal maintenance, an ongoing and substantial change in circumstance must have occurred, which renders the original award unreasonable. Some examples of circumstances that may qualify as an ongoing and substantial change in circumstances include such things as serious illness, loss of employment and inability to secure equivalent employment, and the recipient spouse's ability to support himself or herself through employment.

In Missouri, the former spouse receiving spousal maintenance has a duty to attempt to become self-supporting. Your former spouse's failure to make reasonable attempts to become self-supporting may also, in some circumstances, form the basis for a motion to modify.

11

Division of Property

Whether by settlement or the determination of the judge, all of the assets owned by both you and your spouse will be divided or allocated between you as a result of a divorce. This includes not only the significant assets such as real estate and pensions, but also everyday household items such as dishes and bath towels. Although many assets are easily valued, other assets are more difficult to value. For example, placing a value on a family business or professional practice, or assigning a value to a future pension, may be more difficult and complex endeavors.

With the support of your attorney, you will make strategic decisions concerning which assets may require the involvement of experts on value. There are many factors to consider in deciding how to divide the marital assets including tax consequences and fluctuations in the stock market.

11.1 What system does Missouri use for dividing marital property?

Missouri law provides for an *equitable (fair) division* of the property and debts acquired during your marriage. Regardless of which person owns the property or holds title to the property, the court will divide all of the marital assets and marital debts. In many cases an equitable division may mean an equal division. However the percentages awarded may be disproportionate and still be considered "equitable." Under the Missouri statutes, the court is required to consider a list of factors when deciding upon how to divide the property and debts. These factors may include:

- The current economic circumstances of you and your spouse
- The contribution of each spouse to the acquisition of the marital property
- The contribution of a spouse as homemaker
- The value of non-marital property set aside to each spouse
- The conduct of both parties during the marriage
- The custodial arrangements for the children.

This list is non-exclusive—the court may also consider other factors and also has the discretion to give disproportionate significance to any of the factors at issue in the case.

11.2   What does *community property* mean?

The term *community property* refers to system used in some states, for dividing assets in a divorce. In states having community property laws, each spouse holds a one-half interest in most property acquired during the marriage. Missouri is not a community property state. As such, community property laws do not apply.

11.3   How is it determined who gets the house?

If it is a marital asset, the residence will be included in the division of property. It will be divided either by mutual agreement of the couple through a settlement or by the judge after a trial. Even though the court has the authority to grant one spouse exclusive access to the home while the case is pending, the court does not do this in every case. Even if the court grants one party exclusive access, this action does not determine which party will be awarded the residence at the conclusion of the case.

There are several factors to determine who gets the home:

- Who can afford the mortgage and expenses associated with the home?
- How has the custody of the children been determined?
- Was the house was owned by one of the spouses prior to their marriage?

- Are there are other assets in the marital estate to offset the value of the home?

Talk with your lawyer about your options and the above listed factors.

11.4 Should the house be sold during the divorce proceedings?

In order to sell the marital home while your divorce case is pending, both you and your spouse will need to agree to sell. At the end of the case, the marital home will generally either be awarded to one of the parties or ordered to be sold, with the sale proceeds being divided in some percentage between the parties. When deciding whether you want to ask the court to award you the marital residence, you might want to take into consideration the following:

- The impact on the children if the home is sold
- Whether you can afford to stay in the house after the divorce on your own income plus any support awarded
- Whether there is enough equity in the other marital assets for your spouse to be awarded an equitable share of the marital property if you receive all of the equity in the house
- The cost savings associated with purchasing or renting a smaller or simpler home
- The state of the housing market in your community and current mortgage rates
- Your ability to retain the existing mortgage or need to refinance to remove your spouse from liability on the mortgage

Consider what is important to you in creating your life after divorce when deciding whether to seek to keep your home.

11.5 How do I determine how much our house is worth?

Your home can be one of the most valuable assets that will be divided by the court in your case. Therefore, it is very important that the court get the value correct when it awards the home. In Missouri, courts assign a value to all property, including real estate, based upon its fair market value. If your name is on the title to the property, the court can consider your personal opinion as to the value of the home. However, unless you have training in the field of real estate appraisal, your personal opinion might not carry as much weight if your spouse hires a qualified appraiser to offer his or her opinion of the fair market value of the real estate.

As a practical matter, if you and your spouse can agree on a mutually acceptable value, you can enter into a stipulation that will be binding upon the court. If you do not want to go to the expense of hiring a professional appraiser, you might consider seeking informal guidance from a local real estate agent on the approximate value of your home through a market analysis. Talk to your attorney to determine the best method to value your home in your divorce.

11.6 My house is worth less than what is owed. What are my options?

If you are "upside down" or "underwater" on your home loan, it will likely be treated as a debt, rather than an asset. The trial court must still determine the value of house and its associated debt in the divorce proceeding. Discuss the options available to you to deal with this scenario with your attorney.

If you have reason to think the market for your house will rebound in a reasonable time frame and you are able to pay the monthly mortgage, you may ask the court to award the home to you. It may also be worthwhile to look into other options such as a "short sale."

11.7 What is meant by *equity* in my home?

Equity is the difference between the fair market value of the home and the amount owed in mortgages, liens, or other indebtedness which are recorded against the property.

For example, if the mortgage on the marital home is $50,000 and there is no other indebtedness against the property, the total debt owed against the house is $50,000. If your home has a fair market value of $450,000, the equity in your home totals $400,000. (This is the $450,000 value minus the $50,000 mortgage, which equals $400,000 in equity.)

Unless the court orders the home sold, it will have to take into account the equity in marital residence awarded to one spouse when making its equitable division of marital property. If the equity in the martial home represents a disproportionately large portion of the marital estate, it can be challenging for the court to make an equitable division without ordering a payment from the person receiving the house to the other spouse.

11.8 How will the equity in our house be divided?

If the home is ordered to be sold after the divorce, the equity in the home will most likely be divided at the time of the sale, after the mortgage and other debts have been paid.

If either you or your spouse will be awarded the house, there are a number of options for the other party being compensated for his or her share of the equity in the marital home. These could include:

- The spouse who does not receive the house receives other assets (for example, savings or investment accounts, or other real estate holdings) to offset his or her respective share of the equity. Make sure that you consider the tax implications of the assets you exchange for equity in the house. A dollar of equity in a marital residence is not equal to a dollar contained in a 401(k) due to tax consequences.

- The person who remains in the home agrees to refinance the home to obtain the cash needed to pay the other party his or her share of the equity.

Because the marital residence is a valuable asset, it is important that you and your attorney discuss the details of its disposition. These include:

- The fair market value of the property
- The ability of either party to refinance to remove the other party from liability for the mortgage
- If the house is to be sold, the dates on which certain actions should be taken, such as listing the home for sale, the selection of the real estate agent and the costs for preparing the home for sale
- How mortgage and other joint payments will be made until the house is sold

If you and your spouse do not agree regarding which of you will remain in the home, the court will decide who keeps it or may order the property sold.

11.9 What is a *quitclaim deed,* and how does it affect my former spouse's responsibility with respect to the mortgage?

A *quitclaim deed* is a legal document that transfers one person's interest in property to another person. However, removing your spouse's name from the title of your property will not remove his or her obligation on the mortgage if his or her name is on the loan. Usually, you and your spouse will have signed a contract, or a promissory note, to borrow money from the lender. So, removing your spouse's name from the title on the property, does not remove his or her obligation to repay the money borrowed. To remove your spouse from the obligation, you must refinance the current mortgage or obtain an agreement with the mortgage bank to remove the other spouse from the note.

11.10 Who keeps all the household goods until the decree is signed?

The court will ordinarily not make any decisions about who keeps the household goods while the divorce is pending. Many couples attempt to resolve these issues on their own rather than incur legal fees to dispute household goods. However, if needed, the court may enter an order prohibiting either spouse from transferring, selling, or destroying household goods during the divorce process.

11.11 How can I reduce the risk that assets will be hidden, transferred, or destroyed by my spouse?

Consulting with an attorney before the filing of divorce will help you to take the steps necessary to reduce the risk that assets will be hidden, transferred, or destroyed by your spouse. This is especially important if your spouse has a history of destroying property, incurring substantial debt, or transferring money without your knowledge.

Possible actions you and your attorney may consider include:

- Securing your family heirlooms or other valuables in a safe location
- Preparing an inventory of the personal property
- Taking photographs or video of the property
- Obtaining copies of important records or statements
- Obtaining a restraining order to prevent your spouse from secreting, dissipating, transferring, or destroying property

You should also plan to discuss with your attorney any plans you may have to leave the marital home, so that any actions taken early in your case are consistent with your ultimate goals. Speak candidly with your lawyer about your concerns so that a plan can be developed to provide a level of protection that is appropriate to your circumstances.

11.12 How are assets such as cars, boats, and furniture divided, and when does this happen?

In many cases, spouses are able to reach their own agreements about how to divide personal property, such as household furnishings and vehicles. In those cases where the parties are unable to agree, the court will divide personal property along with all of the other marital assets. Typically, each party will submit a list of personal property and household goods to the court along with a proposed allocation.

Always look to see whether it is a good use of your attorney fees to argue over items of personal property. Items without sentimental value can, for the most part, be easily replaced. The more you and your spouse argue over these types of items, the more it will cost you in legal fees. By the time the divorce is over, you may discover that you spent more in attorney's fees to argue over the items than it would have cost to purchase new items.

11.13 How do I value our used personal property?

In a divorce, your personal property will be valued at its fair market value. The *fair market value* is the price a buyer would be willing to pay for the item in an arms-length transaction. Unless an item is a valuable antique or piece of art, the court will likely assign a value to personal property using garage sale or estate sale prices. For example, if you bought a sofa for $3,000 five years ago, the fair market value of the couch is probably what you could sell it for at a garage sale or on Craigslist today. The fair market value is not what you paid for an item, or how much it will cost to replace it. Instead, the value of your personal property is what you could reasonably sell it for in its current used condition.

11.14 My spouse and I own a coin collection. How will our collection be valued and divided in our divorce?

If you own a unique collection such things as coins, musical instruments, guns, art, or collectibles, talk with your attorney about how to value the collection. It may be that you will need the collection appraised by an expert who has specialized knowledge or experience in determining the value.

If you and your spouse cannot agree on who will keep the collection, it is possible the judge will order the collection to be sold. The judge may also order you to divide the collection between you and your spouse.

11.15 What is meant by a *property inventory* and how detailed should mine be?

A *property inventory* is a listing of the property you own. It may also include a brief description of the property. Discuss with your attorney the level of inventory detail needed to benefit your case.

Factors to consider when creating your inventory may include:

- The extent to which you anticipate you and your spouse will disagree regarding the division of your property
- Whether you anticipate a dispute regarding the value of the property either you or your spouse is retaining
- Whether you will have continued access to the property if a later inventory is needed or whether you spouse will retain control of the property
- Whether you or your spouse are likely to disagree about which items are premarital, inherited, or gifts from someone other than your spouse.

In addition to creating an inventory, your attorney may request that you prepare a list of the property that you and your spouse have already divided or a list of the items you want but your spouse has not agreed to give to you.

If you do not have continued access to your property, talk to your attorney about taking photographs or obtaining access to the property to complete your inventory.

11.16 What happens to our individual checking and savings accounts during and after the divorce?

Regardless of whose name is on a bank account, the account may be considered a marital asset and may be divided by the court. Each party may continue to use their joint or individual financial accounts during the course of the divorce unless a local circuit court rule or restraining order, obtained by one spouse, prevents one or both parties from doing so. Discuss with your attorney how to best handle these accounts while the case is pending.

11.17 How and when are liquid assets such as bank and investment accounts divided?

Whether the case is tried in court or settled by mutual agreement, the dissolution judgment will contain a division of all of the marital assets, including bank and investment accounts. In order to carry out the division, a financial institution will typically require instruction from the divorcing couple. Each financial institution has its own requirements, which range from the receipt of a copy of the relevant portion of the divorce decree to a *medallion signature* (a guarantee by a financial institution that a signature is authentic that also subjects the financial institution to liability for forgery.) However, most financial institutions will accept a letter signed by both parties that contains instructions detailing the allocation of assets. You should inquire in advance of the entry of the dissolution judgment as to the requirements of the financial institutions you use so that you can avoid any unnecessary delays.

11.18 How is pet custody determined?

Possession of pets after divorce is determined on a case-by-case basis. Missouri law is not well established on the matter of the handling of family pets in divorce. However, it is important to know that pets are treated as items of personal property and, as such, the court will not engage in any "best interest" analysis similar to that used in determining the custodial arrangements for children of the marriage. Factors that the court may consider include:

- Who purchased the pet?
- Who provided care for the pet?
- When and why was the pet acquired?
- If there are children, where will the children be? Can the pet travel with the children?

11.19 How will our property in another state be divided?

For the purposes of dividing your assets, out-of-state property is treated the same as property in Missouri. Although a Missouri court cannot order a change in the title to property located in another state, a judge can order your spouse either to turn the property over to you or to sign a deed or other document to transfer title to you.

11.20 What does it mean to *commingle* property?

Commingling occurs when one spouse's separate property is mixed or combined with marital property. The commingling of property, alone, does not convert separate property into marital property. However, it is the burden of the party claiming separate property to trace his or her separate property. If separate property and marital property have been commingled to the point that the separate property can no longer be distinguished from the marital property, the property may be treated by the court as entirely marital property.

11.21 Are all of the assets—such as real property, bank accounts, and inheritances—that I had prior to my marriage still going to be mine after the divorce?

In Missouri, there is a legal presumption that assets acquired during the marriage are marital property, and such property will be included in the assets divided by the court. However, property received as a gift or inheritance, or that you owned before the marriage, is treated as separate property.

Separate property of either spouse is not included in the assets divided by the court in your divorce; it is to be awarded to its owner. It will be your burden to prove with "clear and convincing evidence" the manner of acquisition of your separate property, in order to overcome the presumption of marital property. For example, if you own a vehicle that you brought into the marriage, and can prove ownership, the court will set-aside the vehicle as your separate property.

Missouri law characterizes income earned on separate property during marriage as marital property. As a result, certain separate assets, such as interest bearing accounts may become commingled, (that is, when both marital property and separate property become mixed together within the same account).

Commingling typically occurs as the result of reinvestment of interest and/or dividends within an account that started out as entirely separate. As previously stated, under the current law, commingling alone does not convert separate property into marital property. However, the person claiming a property is separate, must trace out the separate property within the account.

If the account has been so commingled that it is impossible to identify the marital and separate components of the account, the court may deem the entire account to be marital. This is called *transmutation*.

11.22 Will I get to keep my engagement ring?

Yes. Absent other facts, an engagement ring will be treated by the court as a gift and therefore as separate property.

11.23 Can I keep gifts and inheritances I received during the marriage?

The same rules that apply to premarital assets also apply gifts and inheritances received during the marriage. The gifts you receive during the marriage, other than gifts to you and your spouse as a married couple, will be characterized as your separate property and set aside for you. The identity of the gift giver does not matter. As such, even gifts between spouses will be treated as separate property.

When dividing the marital estate, the court may consider the amount of separate property set aside for each spouse as one of the factors in making an equitable distribution of the marital property. The greater the disparity in the amount of separate property owned by each spouse, the greater the chance that this factor could impact the division of marital property.

For example, ignoring all of the other factors, if one spouse has inherited several million dollars and the other has only a few premarital household items, it is more likely that the judge will award the spouse without substantial separate property a greater share of the marital property. However, the judge's consideration of the other relevant factors to property division may counterbalance or even negate the impact of disproportionate amounts of separate property. The court has a great amount of discretion in this determination.

11.24 If my spouse and I can't decide who gets what, who decides? Can one's spouse's decision be contested?

If you and your spouse cannot agree on the division of your property, the judge will make the determination after considering the evidence at your trial. Both parties have the right to appeal the trial court's division of property.

Missouri law affords the trial judge a significant amount of discretion in dividing marital property. Before you file an appeal, you should discuss with your attorney whether you have a legal basis to appeal the property division.

11.25 How are the values of property determined?

The value of some assets, like bank accounts and cars are frequently not disputed. The values of other assets, such as homes or small businesses, are more likely to generate significant disagreement. If your case proceeds to trial, you may give your opinion of the value of property you own. You or your spouse may also elect to have certain property appraised by an expert. In such cases it may be necessary to have the appraiser appear at trial to give testimony regarding the appraisals and or valuations.

If you own substantial assets for which the value is likely to be disputed, talk to your attorney early in your case about the benefits and costs of expert witnesses.

11.26 What does *date of valuation* mean?

The value of assets you own may change while the divorce is pending. This may be the result of your spending from your accounts or the result of market fluctuations. This fact makes property division constantly "fluid" and requires a set date for valuing the marital assets. This is referred to as the *date of valuation.* In Missouri, the court is required to value the property at the date closest to the date of division. This is usually the trial date. However, if a substantial amount of time passes with no judgment, or there is a significant change in value of one or more of your assets, you should discuss with your attorney the possibility of filing a motion to present additional evidence to update values.

11.27 Who gets the interest from certificates of deposit, and dividends from stock holdings during the divorce proceedings?

Interest and dividends are both marital properties to be divided by the court. Whether you or your spouse receives interest from these assets is decided as a part of the overall division of your property and debts.

11.28 Does each one of our financial accounts have to be divided in half if we agree to an equal division of our assets?

No. Rather than incurring the administrative challenges and expense of dividing each asset in half, you and your spouse can decide that one of you will take certain assets equal to the value of assets taken by the spouse. If necessary, one of you can agree to make cash payment to the other to make an equitable division. Make sure that you take into consideration the tax consequences associated with each type of account.

11.29 Is my health savings account an asset that can be divided in the divorce?

Yes. A *health savings account (HSA)* is a tax-advantaged medical savings account to which contributions may be made by employees, employers, or both. Your HSA is an asset to be included in the property distribution and may, depending upon the plan, be divided according to your divorce decree and transferred to another HSA. A division according to a decree does not constitute a distribution and is thus a tax-free transfer.

11.30 I worked very hard for years to support my family while my spouse completed an advanced degree. Do I have a right to any of my spouse's future earnings?

Existing Missouri law does not provide a right to a share of your spouse's future earnings as a consequence of the support you provided while your spouse was earning his or her degree. You may, however, be a candidate for spousal maintenance if you are unable to meet your reasonable needs on your income alone.

Additionally, your contributions during the marriage, including your contribution to your spouse's ability to obtain the advanced degree, are factors to be considered in the division of the property. It will also to be considered in the determination of spousal maintenance. Be sure to give your attorney a complete history of your contributions to the marriage and the earning capacity of your spouse. Ask about their potential impact on the outcome of your case.

11.31 How will the court treat our business or professional practice?

A business or professional practice is an asset in divorce, and at the same time, it may have many unique attributes. If you or your spouse own a business, it is important that you work with your attorney early in your case to develop a strategy for valuing the business and making your case for how it should be treated in the division of property and debts.

The valuation of such interests can become complex. This often is based upon whether the business has an element of intangible value, or what we call "goodwill." This means a value in excess of the identifiable, tangible assets of the business or practice. For instance, many businesses have tangible assets such as money in the bank, equipment, inventory, and real estate. However, sometimes the value in the business is represented by the professional skills of the owner. What value do these skills have to a buyer? Where the value of the business is highly dependent upon the individual skills of the professional, there may be little to "sell" and the business or practice may not

169

be readily transferrable to a potential buyer. Missouri has a very robust body of law addressing these issues. Consult your lawyer about how the law applies to your situation.

11.32 My spouse and I have owned and run our own business together for many years. Can I be forced out of it?

Yes. One of the goals of the court is to sever the marital relationship, which can include joint business ventures. Deciding what should happen with a family business when divorce occurs can be particularly challenging.

In discussing your options with your lawyer, consider the following questions:

- If one spouse retains ownership of the business, are there enough other assets for the other spouse to receive a fair share of the total marital assets?
- Which spouse has the skills and experience to continue running the business?
- What would you do if you weren't working in the business?
- What is the value of the business?
- What is the market for the business if it were to be sold?
- Could you remain an employee of the business for some period of time even if you were not an owner?

If you have truly been jointly responsible for the success of your family business, you and your spouse know your business best. With the help of your lawyers, you may be able to create a settlement that can satisfy you both. If not, the judge will make the decision for you at trial.

11.33 I suspect my spouse is hiding assets, but I can't prove it. How can I protect myself if I discover later that I was right?

After your divorce, if you learn that your spouse hid assets from you and the court, you will have the ability to file a separate lawsuit to request that the court divide the hidden assets. If you reach a settlement, ask your lawyer to include language in the settlement documents to address your concerns about hidden assets. This might be accomplished by including an acknowledgment by your spouse that the agreement was based upon a full and complete disclosure of his or her financial condition.

11.34 My spouse says I'm not entitled to a share of his stock options because he gets to keep them only if he stays employed with his company. What are my rights?

Stock options are often very valuable assets. They are also one of the more complex issues when dividing assets during a divorce for these reasons:

- Each company has its own rules about awarding and exercising stock options.
- Complete information is needed from the employer.
- There are different methods for calculating the value of stock options.
- The reasons the options were given can impact the valuation and division. For example, some are given for future performance and may be considered separate property.
- There are cost and tax considerations when options are exercised.

Generally, even if they have not yet vested, stock options and similar awards are marital property in Missouri and may be allocated between the parties if the attorneys or the court address the complexities involved. If either you or your spouse owns stock options or similar employment benefits or awards, begin discussing this asset with your attorney early in your case to allow sufficient time to settle the issues or to be well prepared for trial.

11.35 What is a *prenuptial agreement* and how might it affect the property settlement phase of the divorce?

A *prenuptial agreement,* sometimes referred to as a *premarital* or *antenuptial agreement,* is a contract entered into between two people prior to their marriage which can include provisions for how assets and debts will be divided in the event the marriage is terminated as well as provisions regarding maintenance. In this way, the parties to a prenuptial agreement can modify how the law would otherwise treat them in the

171

event of their divorce or death. Your property settlement is likely to be impacted by the terms of your prenuptial agreement if the court enforces the agreement.

11.36 Can a prenuptial agreement be contested during the divorce?

Yes. Because of the special relationship of trust between two people who intend to marry, the negotiation of their prenuptial agreement requires many elements and protections that are not necessarily required with respect to the negotiation and finalization of other contracts.

The two spouses must enter into the prenuptial agreement freely, fairly, and with a complete mutual disclosure of their respective assets and liabilities. Each person must be provided sufficient opportunity to consult with counsel not only about the legal impact of the agreement but also so that they understand the rights that they would have had without the agreement.

The parties to such an agreement must also have been accorded sufficient time in advance of its execution to allow them a reasonable and meaningful opportunity to consider and negotiate the terms of the agreement. Accordingly, in deciding whether to enforce the agreement, the court may consider many factors. Among them are:

- Whether your agreement was entered into voluntarily
- Whether your agreement was conscionable at the time it was signed
- Whether you and your spouse made a complete disclosure of your assets, debts and income
- Whether you and your spouse each had your own lawyer
- Whether you and your spouse each had enough time to consider and negotiate the agreement
- Whether your spouse has breached any of the terms of the prenuptial agreement
- Whether you are each receiving something in the agreement, in exchange for what you may be giving up

If you have a prenuptial agreement, bring a copy of it to the initial consultation with your attorney. Be sure to provide your lawyer with a detailed history of the facts and circumstances surrounding reaching and signing the agreement.

11.37 I'm Jewish and want my husband to cooperate with obtaining a *get,* which is a religious divorce. Can I get a court order for this?

Talk to your lawyer about obtaining a *get cooperation clause* in your divorce decree, including a provision regarding who should pay for it.

11.38 Who will get the frozen embryo of my egg and my spouse's sperm that we have stored at a health clinic?

This question involves a complex and evolving area of the law. The terms of your contract with the clinic may impact the rights you and your spouse may have to the embryo, so provide a copy of it to your attorney for review.

11.39 Will debts be considered when determining the division of the property?

Yes. The court must consider any debts incurred during the course of the marriage when dividing the property. For example, if you are awarded a car valued at $12,000, but you owe a $10,000 debt on the same vehicle, the court will take that debt into consideration in the overall division of the assets. Similarly, if one spouse is ordered to pay substantial marital credit card debt, the court may take that obligation into consideration when making its final determination of the division of property.

11.40 What is a *settlement agreement?*

A *settlement agreement* is a written document that includes all of the relevant settlement terms, including the financial agreements you and your spouse have reached in your divorce. These financial terms will include the division of property, debts, child support, maintenance, insurance, and attorney fees.

The settlement may be a separate document, or it may be incorporated into the decree of dissolution, which is the final court order dissolving your marriage. If you elect to incorporate the terms of the settlement agreement in the decree of dissolution, those terms will have the weight and force of a judgment and may be enforced with contempt proceedings.

11.41 What happens after my spouse and I approve the property settlement agreement? Do we still have to go to court?

Not necessarily. Your judge must still approve the settlement agreement and decree after both you and your spouse sign. If you choose, the judge can approve your decree at a final hearing known as a *non-contested hearing*. A non-contested hearing can be scheduled after the passing of the thirty-day mandatory waiting period after under Missouri law, assuming you and your spouse have also resolved all matters pertaining to your minor children.

If you and your spouse reach a property settlement agreement, a court date for your final hearing can often be obtained earlier than a trial date, because a non-contested hearing requires significantly less time than a trial. However, a non-contested hearing may not be required. As an alternative to a non-contested hearing, your judge may allow you to submit your judgment and all related settlement documents along with an affidavit for the judge to approve without you or your spouse having to go to court.

11.42 If my spouse and I think our property settlement agreement is fair, why does the judge have to approve it?

Under Missouri law, the judge has a duty to ensure that all property settlement agreements in divorces are "not unconscionable" (that is, an inequality so strong, gross, and manifest that it must be impossible to state it to one with common sense without producing an exclamation at the inequality of it). For this reason, your judge must review and approve your agreement before it can be considered to be binding upon either party.

11.43 What happens to the property distribution if one of us dies before the divorce proceedings are completed?

A Missouri divorce case ceases immediately upon the death of either spouse. As such, if your spouse dies prior to your divorce decree being entered, the divorce will not proceed to conclusion, and you will be considered married and treated as a surviving spouse under the law.

11.44 After our divorce is final, can the property agreement be modified?

Generally, provisions in your property settlement agreement or decree dealing with the distribution of your assets and debts are not modifiable. Without an uncommon instance of fraud or duress, the property settlement agreement cannot be modified.

12

Benefits: Insurance, Retirement, and Pensions

During your marriage, both you and your spouse likely benefited from the fringe benefits of one another. Most frequently, these benefits take the form of health insurance for an employee that is also made available to his or her dependents, and participation in some form of employer sponsored retirement plan. While you may have taken the existence of these benefits for granted, it is important to take into consideration your rights with respect to these benefits during the course of your divorce.

After you divorce, some benefits that arose out of your spouse's employment will terminate, some may continue for a period of time, and others may be divided between you. Retirement assets, in particular, often represent one of the most valuable marital assets to be divided in a divorce.

Whether the benefits are from your employer or from your spouse's, with your attorney's help you will develop a better understanding of which benefits the law considers to be "yours" "mine," and "ours" for continuing or dividing.

12.1 Will my children continue to have health coverage through my spouse's work even though we're divorcing?

According to Missouri law, if at the time of the filing of the petition for divorce either you or your spouse provides health insurance for your children, whichever one of you provides the insurance will be prohibited from cancelling coverage during the pendency of the divorce. Although the court does not have to make either parent obtain health insurance for the parties' children, it is highly likely that the court will require one of the parties to maintain health insurance for the benefit of each child of the marriage until they reach legal age. The cost of health insurance for the children will be taken into consideration in calculating the child support.

12.2 Will I continue to have health insurance through my spouse's work after the divorce?

Most insurers treat divorce as a reason to terminate coverage for a former spouse. Because different insurers have different policies regarding this issue, you will need to investigate the grace period to find out how quickly you will need to obtain new coverage.

Once your coverage through your former spouse terminates, you will need to obtain coverage elsewhere. In most cases, under the federal law known as *COBRA,* you have the right to continue on your spouse's employer-provided plan for up to three years. However, the cost of COBRA can be very high, so you may also wish to investigate obtaining a new health insurance policy through the *Affordable Care Act's* marketplace.

Begin early to investigate your eligibility for coverage on your spouse's health insurance plan after the entry of the decree and your options for your future health insurance. The cost of your health care is an important factor when pursuing spousal support and planning your postdivorce budget.

12.3 What is a *QMSO?*

A *qualified medical support order (QMSO)* is a court order providing continued group health insurance coverage for a minor child. A QMSO may also enable a parent to obtain other information about the plan, without having to go through the parent who has the coverage. Rather than allowing only the parent with the insurance to be reimbursed for a claim, under a QMSO, a health insurance plan is required to reimburse directly whoever actually paid the child's medical expense. QMSO's had a brief period of popularity and common usage, but they are rarely used today; they have been replaced by other laws and practices by health insurance providers.

12.4   What is a *qualified domestic relations order?*

A *qualified domestic relations order (QDRO)* is a court order that requires a retirement or pension plan administrator pay you the share of your former spouse's retirement that was awarded to you in the decree. A QDRO is only required for retirement and pension plans that are ERISA qualified and are unnecessary to divide a retirement account such as an IRA.

Other types of retirement plans, such as the federal Civil Service Retirement System or military retirement benefits require different types of orders in order to effectuate the terms of the divorce judgment.

Obtaining a QDRO is a critical step in the divorce process. They can be complex documents, and a number of steps are required to reduce future concerns about enforcement and to fully protect your rights. These court orders must comply with numerous technical rules and be approved by the plan administrator, which is often located outside of Missouri.

Whenever possible, court orders dividing retirement plans should be entered at or near the same time as the entry of the decree of divorce.

12.5   How many years must I have been married before I'm eligible to receive a part of my spouse's retirement fund or pension?

No minimum duration exists in order for you to qualify for an interest in your spouse's retirement plan or pension. As long as your spouse contributed to or participated in the plan during some portion of your marriage, at least some portion of your spouse's retirement will be characterized as marital property.

The size of your interest will depend upon two primary factors depending on the type of plan. For defined contribution retirement plans, such as a 401(k), the greater the level of contribution to the plan during the marriage, the greater the marital interest. For defined benefit retirement plans, such as a traditional pension, the greater the amount of time your spouse participated in the plan during the marriage, the greater the marital interest.

12.6 I contributed to my retirement plan for ten years before I got married. Will my spouse get half of my entire pension?

No. As with all property acquired prior to marriage, a person's interest in his or premarital pension contributions remains his or her separate property. If either you or your spouse made premarital contributions to a pension or retirement plan, make sure to let your attorney know.

Because the party asserting the existence of separate property has the burden of proving its separate nature, you must gather the supporting documentation to show the dates of your participation and contributions. This is information essential to determine the marital and non-marital portions of the retirement plan.

12.7 I plan to keep my same job after my divorce. Will my former spouse get half of the money I contribute to my retirement plan after my divorce?

No, not unless you agree to do so voluntarily. All of the money that you earn for work done after the divorce remains your separate (nonmarital) property. Your former spouse does not have any rights to property other than property accumulated during the marriage. For retirement assets such as pensions, the participant may continue to accrue additional benefits after the divorce. The court is equipped to deal with scenarios such as this by utilizing a formula that awards the ex-spouse only a percentage of the pension that accrued during the marriage.

You can assist your attorney by obtaining copies of the retirement plans in which you have an interest. If you know that your plan differs from the ordinary 401(k), SEP or 403(b), you should inform your attorney so that the language of the court order ensures protection of your postdivorce retirement contributions.

12.8 Am I still entitled to a share of my spouse's retirement even though I never contributed to a plan during our twenty-five-year-year marriage?

Yes. Retirement plans are often the most valuable asset accumulated during a marriage. Consequently, your judge will consider the retirement along with all of the other marital assets and debts when determining a fair division. However, it is important to understand that the critical element is that the court counts the retirement as part of a marital estate. If the trial court includes the value of the retirement asset in the marital estate and awards one party the entire retirement plan, the other party will receive equivalent value via other marital assets.

12.9 My lawyer says I'm entitled to a share of my spouse's retirement. How can I find out how much I get and when I'm eligible to receive it?

More than one factor will determine your rights to collect from your spouse's retirement. One factor will be the terms of the court order dividing the retirement. The court order will tell you whether you are entitled to a set dollar amount, a percentage, or a fraction to be determined based upon the length of your marriage and how long your spouse continues working.

For a defined benefit plan, such as a pension, the fraction used by the court to determine how much you are eligible to receive will usually be the number of years you were married while your spouse was employed at that company divided by the total number of years your spouse is employed with the company.

Another factor will be the terms of the retirement plan itself. Some provide for lump-sum withdrawals; others issue payments in monthly installments. Review both the terms of your court order and contact the plan administrator to obtain the clearest understanding of your rights and benefits.

12.10 If I am eligible to receive my spouse's retirement benefits, when am I eligible to begin collecting them? Do I have to be sixty-five to collect them?

The answer depends upon the terms of your spouse's retirement plan. In some cases it is possible to begin receiving your share at the earliest date your spouse is eligible to receive them, regardless of whether he or she elects to do so. To learn your options, ask your lawyer to obtain documents that describe the terms of your spouse's plan.

12.11 What happens if my former spouse is old enough to receive benefits but I'm not?

Ordinarily you will be eligible to begin receiving your share of the benefits when your former spouse begins receiving his or hers. Depending upon the plan, you may be eligible to elect to receive them sooner.

12.12 Am I entitled to *cost-of-living increases* on my share of my spouse's retirement?

It depends. Some, but certainly not all pension plans include what is known as a *cost-of-living adjustment (COLA)*. A COLA serves to adjust the amount of the annual pension benefit to compensate for increases in the cost of living. Typically, the amount of the increase is tied to a benchmark, such as the consumer price index. If your spouse has a retirement plan that includes a provision for a COLA, talk to your lawyer about whether this can be included in the court order dividing the retirement.

12.13 What circumstances might prevent me from receiving part of my spouse's retirement benefits?

Some pension plans, if they are in lieu of a Social Security benefit, are, by Missouri law not subject to division in a divorce proceeding. For example, the Missouri public teacher's pension is not divisible in divorce, regardless of the fact that it was accumulated during the marriage. If you or your spouse are employed by a government agency, talk with your lawyer about whether you are entitled to any other retirement benefits, and determine how this may affect the property settlement in your case.

12.14 Does the death of my spouse affect the payout of retirement benefits to me or to our children?

It depends upon both the nature of your spouse's retirement plan and the terms of the court order dividing the retirement. If you want to be eligible for survivorship benefits from your spouse's pension, discuss the issue with your attorney before your case is settled or goes to trial. He or she can advise you.

Divorce in Missouri

Some plans allow only a surviving spouse or former spouse to be a beneficiary. Others may allow for the naming of an alternate beneficiary, such as your children.

12.15 Can I still collect on my former spouse's Social Security benefits if he or she passes on before I do?

It depends. You may be eligible to receive benefits if:

- You were married to your spouse for ten or more years
- You are not remarried
- You are at least sixty-two years old
- The benefit you would receive based on your own earning record is less than the benefit you would receive from your former spouse

For more information, contact your local Social Security Administration office or visit the SSA website at www.ssa.gov.

12.16 What orders might the court enter regarding life insurance?

In addition to its power to divide life insurance policies with cash value as marital property, the court has the authority to order you or your spouse to maintain a life insurance policy to ensure future spousal maintenance payments.

However, the same does not hold true for child support payments. Even though a couple may agree in a negotiated settlement to require one parent to maintain life insurance on him or herself as security for child support, Missouri courts are prohibited from issuing such orders in a case that proceeds to trial.

You will be required to pay for your own life insurance after your divorce, and you should include this as an expense when you prepare your statement of income and expense.

12.17 Because we share children, should I consider my spouse as a beneficiary on my life insurance?

This decision is entirely up to you. However, it is important to realize that making your former spouse the beneficiary of your life insurance proceeds does not offer any protection for your children. If your intent is to make sure that your children are provided for after your death, you might want to consider making a trust for your children the beneficiary of the policy. You can name your former spouse or other trusted individual as the trustee to manage the death benefit for your children. Discuss what options are available to you with your attorney.

12.18 Can the court require in the decree that I be the beneficiary of my spouse's insurance policy, as long as the children are minors or indefinitely?

Although you can certainly agree in a settlement to remain the beneficiary of your spouse's life insurance policy, the court cannot do the same on its own accord. In Missouri, the court does not have the power to require one spouse to maintain life insurance benefits for an ex-spouse for the purpose of making up for future lost child support.

12.19 My spouse is in the military. What are my rights to benefits after the divorce?

As the former spouse of a military member, the types of benefits to which you may be entitled are typically determined by the number of years you were married, the number of years your spouse was in the military while you were married, and whether or not you have remarried. Be sure you obtain accurate information about these dates.

Among the benefits for which you may be eligible are:

- A portion of your spouse's military retirement pay
- A survivor benefit in the event of your spouse's death
- Health care or participation in a temporary, transitional health care program
- Ability to keep your military identification card
- Use of certain military facilities, such as the commissary

Although your divorce is pending, educate yourself about your right to future military benefits so that you can plan for your future with clarity. If your divorce is still pending, contact your base legal office, or for more information, visit the website for the branch of the military of which your spouse was a member.

Also, consider consulting a family law attorney who is familiar the various attributes of military benefits in divorce. The rules are complex and specialized and specific orders and deadlines apply.

13

Division of Debts

In the same manner that the court must divide marital property between spouses, it must also divide all marital debts. These debts can range anywhere from substantial obligations such as mortgages and IRS debt to credit card balances and store charges. Frequently the debts at issue are intimately tied to specific assets, which leads to a logical allocation. It only makes sense to obligate the spouse that is awarded the family boat with the loan the parties used to finance its purchase. Other debts, such as credit card debt may prove more challenging to allocate.

There are steps you can take to ensure the best outcome possible when it comes to dividing your marital debt. These include providing accurate and complete debt information to your lawyer and updating that information as it changes throughout the course of the divorce.

13.1 Who is responsible for paying ordinary household expenses during the divorce proceedings?

At the beginning of a divorce case, many issues, such as the payment of the mortgage, utilities, and credit card payments remain unclear. This is especially true when the recurring obligations are in joint names. The trial court can order temporary maintenance and allocate which party will be responsible for certain expenses. The court also has the power to enter a restraining order preventing one or both parties from "disposing of any property except in the usual course of business or for the necessities of life."

In most cases, the court will not make decisions (on a temporary basis) regarding the payment of discretionary credit card debt. It is important to discuss with your attorney a plan to address credit card spending and payment of monthly balances to prevent spending from getting out of hand. If both spouses neglect to make at least minimum payments on time, the marital estate will suffer due to substantial finance charges and late fees. The court will divide all of the marital debts, including credit card debt.

In Missouri, the purpose of temporary orders is to preserve the *status quo*. That means the court in implementing temporary orders, takes the parties as it finds them, including their present earning, if any. As a result, typically the spouse who remains in the home will be responsible for the mortgage payments, taxes, utilities, and most other ordinary expenses.

However, if the spouse remaining in the home does not work or has insufficient income to cover these expenses, the court may award that spouse temporary maintenance. If you are concerned that you cannot afford to stay in the marital home on a temporary basis, talk with your attorney about your options prior to your temporary hearing.

13.2 What, if anything, should I be doing with the credit card companies as we go through the divorce?

If possible, it is a good idea to obtain some credit in your name alone prior to the divorce. This will help you establish credit in your own name and help you with necessary purchases following a separation.

It is also never a bad idea to know your credit score. Begin by obtaining a copy of your credit report from at least two of the three nationwide consumer reporting companies: Experian, Equifax, or TransUnion. The *Fair Credit Reporting Act* entitles you to a free copy of your credit report from each of these three companies every twelve months. To order your free annual report online, go to www.annualcreditreport.com, call toll-free to (877) 322-8228, or complete an Annual Credit Report Request Form and mail it to: Annual Credit Report Request Service, P.O. Box 105281, Atlanta, Georgia 30348-5281. You can print the form from the Federal Trade Commission website at www.ftc.gov/credit.

Your spouse may have incurred debt as an authorized user of credit that is in your name. This information is important to relay to your attorney. If you and your spouse have joint credit card accounts or if your spouse is a authorized user on any of your accounts discuss your options with your attorney.

13.3   How is credit card debt divided?

Credit card debt, just like all other marital debts, will be equitably divided by the court as a part of the overall division of the marital property and debts. If your spouse has exclusively used a credit card for purposes that did not benefit the family, such as gambling, or gifts for a new significant other, let your attorney know. Such expenditures may be treated as squandered assets. In most cases, the court will not review a lengthy history of how you and your spouse used the credit cards, but there can be exceptions.

13.4   Am I responsible for repayment of my spouse's student loans?

It depends. If your spouse incurred student loans prior to the marriage, they are separate debts, which will be set-aside to your spouse.

If the debt was incurred during the marriage, how the funds were used may have an impact on who is ordered to pay them. For example, if your spouse borrowed $3000 during the marriage for tuition, it is likely your spouse will be ordered to pay that debt. However, if your spouse took out $3000 in student loans, but used $1000 of it for a family vacation, the court would be more likely to order the debt shared. These are not absolute rules. The court has a wide degree of discretion in dividing all marital debts, including student loans, so long as its division is appropriate under the circumstances.

If you were a joint borrower on your spouse's student loan and your spouse fails to pay the loan, the lender may attempt to collect from you even if your spouse has been ordered to pay the debt. If either you or your spouse has student loan debt, be sure to give your attorney the complete history regarding the debt and ask about the most likely outcome under the facts of your case.

13.5 During the divorce proceedings, am I still responsible for debt my spouse continues to accrue?

The debts that you and your spouse accrue between the time of filing and the date the divorce judgment is entered will be characterized as marital debts. So long as these expenditures are made on ordinary and reasonable expenses, the court will divide the debt.

13.6 During the marriage my spouse applied for and received several credit cards without my knowledge. Am I responsible for them?

As with all other marital debt, the court will look at the nature of the expenditure, along with the overall fairness of the property and debt division. If your spouse bought items with the cards and intends to keep those items, it is likely that she or he will be ordered to pay the debt associated with the purchases.

The credit card companies are unlikely to be able to pursue collection from you for your spouse's nonpayment of the debt unless your spouse used them for the necessities of life, such as food, necessary clothing, or housing.

13.7 During our marriage, we paid off thousands of dollars of debt incurred by my spouse before we were married. Will the court take this into consideration when dividing our property and debt?

Just as premarital assets can have an impact on the overall division of property and debts, so can premarital debt. Depending upon the length of the marriage, the evidence of the debt, and the amount paid, it may be a factor for the judge to consider. Be sure to let your attorney know if either you or your spouse brought substantial debt into the marriage.

13.8 Regarding debts, what is a hold-harmless/ indemnification clause, and why should it be in the divorce decree?

A *hold-harmless/indemnification provision* is intended to protect you in the event that your spouse fails to follow a court order to pay a debt after the divorce is granted. The language typically provides that your spouse shall "indemnify and hold [you] harmless from liability" on the debt.

187

The court does not have the authority to alter the contractual relationship that you and your spouse have with a creditor. Therefore, if you and your spouse have a joint debt that your spouse fails to pay despite the terms of the judgment, the creditor may attempt to collect from you.

In the event your spouse fails to pay a court-ordered debt and the creditor attempts collection from you, the hold harmless/indemnification provision in your divorce decree can be used in an effort to cause the payment to be made by your former spouse.

13.9 Why do my former spouse's doctors say they have a legal right to collect from me when my former spouse was ordered to pay her own medical bills?

You may be held liable for the "necessities of life" of your spouse, such as health care. Your divorce decree does not take away the legal rights of creditors to collect debts that were incurred during the marriage. Contact your attorney about your rights to enforce the court order that your spouse pays his or her own medical bills.

13.10 My spouse and I have agreed that I will keep our home. Why must I refinance the mortgage?

There may be a number of reasons why your spouse is asking you to refinance the mortgage. First, the mortgage company cannot be forced to take your spouse's name off of the mortgage note. This means that if you did not make the house payments, the lender could pursue collection against your spouse.

Second, your spouse may want to receive their share of the home equity. It may be possible for you to borrow additional money at the time of refinancing to pay your spouse his or her share of the equity in the home.

Third, the mortgage on your family home may prevent your spouse from qualifying for a new mortgage in the future. Because there remains a risk that your spouse could be pursued for the debt to the mortgage company, a second lender may be unwilling to take the risk of extending further credit to your spouse.

13.11 Can I file for bankruptcy while my divorce is pending?

Yes. Consult with your attorney if you are considering filing for bankruptcy while your divorce is pending. It will be important for you to ask yourself a number of questions, such as:

- Should I file for bankruptcy on my own or with my spouse?
- How will filing for bankruptcy affect my credit in the future?
- Which debts can be discharged in bankruptcy, and which cannot?
- How will a bankruptcy affect the division of property and debts in the divorce?
- How might a delay in the divorce proceeding due to a bankruptcy impact my case?
- What form of bankruptcy is best for my situation?

If you use a different attorney for your bankruptcy than you have for your divorce, be sure that each attorney is kept fully informed about the developments in the other case.

13.12 What happens if my spouse files for bankruptcy during our divorce?

Contact your attorney right away. The filing of a bankruptcy while your divorce is pending can have a significant impact on your divorce. Your attorney can advise you whether certain debts are likely to be discharged in the bankruptcy, the delay a bankruptcy may cause to your divorce, and whether bankruptcy is an appropriate option for you.

13.13 Can I file for divorce while I am in bankruptcy?

Yes, however, you must receive the bankruptcy court's permission to proceed with the divorce. Although in bankruptcy, your property is protected from debt collection by the "automatic stay." The stay can also prevent the divorce court from dividing property between you and your spouse until you obtain the bankruptcy court's permission to proceed with the divorce.

13.14 What should I do if my former spouse files for bankruptcy after our divorce?

Contact your attorney immediately. If you learn that your former spouse has filed for bankruptcy, you may have certain rights to object to the discharge of any debts your spouse was ordered to pay under your divorce decree. If you fail to take action, it is possible that you will be held responsible for debts your spouse was ordered to pay.

13.15 If I am awarded child support or maintenance in my decree, can these obligations be discharged if my former spouse files for bankruptcy after our divorce?

No. Support obligations such as child support and maintenance are not dischargeable in bankruptcy, meaning these debts cannot be eliminated in a bankruptcy proceeding.

13.16 What happens if my former spouse does not pay their obligations in the decree?

If your former spouse does not pay the debts assigned to him or her in the decree, you may be able to pursue a contempt of court action. A party is in *contempt of court* if they willfully disobey or disregard a court order. Talk with your attorney to determine whether a contempt of court action may be filed in your case to enforce your rights under your decree.

14

Taxes

A number of tax issues may arise in your divorce. Because most family law attorneys do not specialize in tax, your attorney may not be able to answer all of your tax related questions. Accordingly, consulting with your accountant or tax advisor for advice above and beyond that which your attorney can provide, may be helpful.

Because taxes are such an important consideration in both settlement negotiations and trial preparation, they should not be overlooked. Tax implications will impact many of your decisions, including those regarding maintenance, division of property, and the receipt of benefits.

No one wants a letter from their CPA, or worse, the Internal Revenue Service indicating that they owe more taxes than anticipated. Therefore, taking the time and employing the resources needed to accurately assess the tax implications raised by various aspects of your divorce will pay off in the long run.

14.1 Will either my spouse or I have to pay income tax when we transfer property or pay a property settlement to one another according to our divorce decree?

No. As a general matter, the transfers of property between ex-spouses incident to a divorce do not trigger any federal or state income taxes. However, that does not mean you should ignore the issues of taxes or future taxes when negotiating a settlement. Certain assets have different tax implications down the road that you should discuss with your attorney.

191

14.2   Is the amount of child support I pay tax deductible?

As of the date of the publication of this book, child support paid is not tax deductible.

14.3   Must I pay income tax on any child support I receive?

As of the date of the publication of this book, the child support you receive is tax-free.

14.4   What does the IRS consider alimony?

In Missouri, spousal support is called *maintenance,* and may qualify for tax treatment as alimony under the Internal Revenue Code in certain circumstances. Amounts paid under a divorce decree or according to a written separation agreement entered into between you and your spouse will be considered alimony if:

- You and your spouse or former spouse do not file a joint return with each other
- The payment is in cash (including checks or money orders)
- The payment is received by (or on behalf of) your spouse or former spouse
- You and your former spouse are not members of the same household when you make the payment
- You have no liability to make the payment (in cash or property) after the death of your spouse or former spouse
- Your payment is not treated as child support or a property settlement

Not all payments made according to a divorce or separation decree qualify as alimony or maintenance. Alimony or maintenance does not include:

- Child support
- Noncash property settlements
- Payments to keep up the payor's property
- Use of the payor's property

14.5 Is the amount of maintenance I am ordered to pay tax deductible?

As of the date of the publication of this book, spousal support paid according to a court order is deductible. This will include court-ordered maintenance and may also include other forms of support provided to your former spouse (but not child support). Because your spouse, not you, will be paying taxes on the maintenance you pay, this savings must be considered when determining the amount of maintenance you are willing to offer.

14.6 Must I pay tax on the maintenance I receive?

Yes. You must pay income tax on the spousal support you receive. This will include court-ordered maintenance and may also include other forms of spousal support, but not child support, paid by your spouse.

Income tax is a critical factor in determining an adequate amount of maintenance. Because you pay your expenses with after tax dollars, it is critical to take this fact into consideration when determining how much maintenance to request. If you neglect to consider the taxability of maintenance, you may wind up with a maintenance award insufficient to meet your needs.

If your case proceeds to trial, you will need to present evidence to the court concerning the impact of income tax on the maintenance award. Frequently, one or both sides will hire an expert witness, such as an accountant, to provide this important information.

It is always a good idea to consult with your tax advisor about how to handle the taxes on your spousal support, especially in the first year. Making estimated tax payments throughout the year or withholding additional taxes from your wages could help you avoid a burdensome tax liability at tax time.

14.7 Is there anything else I should know about alimony/maintenance and taxes?

If your maintenance payments to your spouse decrease or end during the first three calendar years after your divorce, you may be subject to the *recapture rule*. You are subject to the recapture rule if the maintenance you pay in the third calender year decreases by more than $15,000 from the second calendar year or maintenance you pay in the second and third year decreases significantly from the maintenance you pay in the first calendar year. If you are subject to this rule, you must claim a portion of the maintenance payments you've previously deducted as income in the third year. Likewise, the recipient can deduct part of the maintenance payments he or she previously claimed as income in the third year.

14.8 During the divorce proceedings, is our tax filing status affected?

It can be. You cannot file as married if your decree is final by December 31 of the applicable tax year. If you are considered unmarried, your filing status is either "single" or, under certain circumstances, "head of household." If your decree is not final as of December 31, your filing status is either "married filing a joint return" or "married filing a separate return," unless you live apart from your spouse and meet the exception for "head of household."

While your divorce is in progress, talk to both your tax advisor and your attorney about your filing status. It may be beneficial to calculate your tax on both a joint return and a separate return to see which gives you the lower tax. IRS Publication 504 Divorced or Separated Individuals, provides more detail on tax issues while you are going through a divorce, and is readily available online.

14.9 Should I file a joint income tax return with my spouse while our divorce is pending?

Consult your tax advisor to determine the risks and benefits of filing a joint return with your spouse. Compare this with the consequences of filing your tax return separately. Often the overall tax liability will be less with the filing of a joint return, but other factors are important to consider, such as joint liability.

When deciding whether to file a joint return with your spouse, consider any concerns you have about the accuracy and truthfulness of the information on the tax return. If you have any doubts, consult both your attorney and your tax advisor before agreeing to sign a joint tax return with your spouse. Prior to filing a return with your spouse, try to reach agreement about how any tax owed or refund expected will be shared, and ask your lawyer to assist you in getting this in writing.

14.10 My spouse will not cooperate in providing the necessary documents to prepare or file our taxes jointly. What options do I have?

Talk with your attorney about requesting your spouse cooperate in the preparation and filing of your joint return. Although a judge cannot order your spouse to sign a joint return, he or she can take your spouse's unreasonable refusal to do so into account in the equitable division of property in some cases.

14.11 For tax purposes, is one time of year better to divorce than another?

It depends upon your tax situation. If you and your spouse agree that it would be beneficial to file joint tax returns for the year in which you are divorcing, you may wish to not have your divorce finalized before the end of the year.

Your marital status for filing income taxes is determined by your status on December 31. Consequently, if you both want to preserve your right to file a joint return, your decree should not be entered before December 31 of that year.

14.12 What tax consequences should I consider regarding the sale of our home?

When your home is sold, whether during your divorce or after, the sale may be subject to a *capital gains tax*. If your home was your primary residence and you lived in the home for two of the preceding five years, you may be eligible to exclude up to $250,000 of the gain on the sale of your home. If both you and your spouse meet the ownership and residence tests, you may be eligible to exclude up to $500,000 of the gain.

If you anticipate the gain on the sale of your residence to be over $250,000, talk with your attorney early in the divorce process about a plan to minimize the tax liability. For more information, see IRS Publication 523 Selling Your Home, or visit the IRS website at www.irs.gov and talk with your tax advisor.

14.13 How might capital gains tax be a problem for me years after the divorce?

Future capital gains tax on the sale of property should be discussed with your attorney during the negotiation and trial preparation stages of your case. This is especially important if the sale of the property is imminent. Failure to do so may result in an unfair outcome.

For example, suppose you agree that your spouse will be awarded the proceeds from the sale of your home valued at $200,000, after the real estate commission, and you will take the stock portfolio also valued at $200,000.

Suppose that after the divorce, you decide to sell the stock. It is still valued at $200,000, but you learn that its original price was $120,000 and that you must pay capital gains tax of 15 percent on the $80,000 of gain. You pay tax of $12,000, leaving you with $188,000.

Meanwhile, your former spouse sells the marital home but pays no capital gains tax because he qualifies for the $250,000 exemption. He is left with the full $200,000.

Tax implications of your property division should always be discussed with your attorney, with support from your tax advisor as needed.

14.14 During and after the divorce, who gets to claim the children as dependents?

This issue should be addressed in settlement negotiations or at trial, if settlement is not reached. The judge has discretion to determine which parent will be entitled to claim the children as exemptions for income tax purposes. The *Missouri Child Support Guidelines* state that one of its assumptions is that the spouse receiving child support also gets to claim the children as exemptions for income tax purposes. If one party has income so low or so high that he or she will not benefit from the dependency exemption, the court may award the exemption to the other parent.

Taxes

14.15 My decree says I have to sign IRS Form 8332 so my former spouse can claim our child as an exemption, because I have custody. Should I sign it once for all future years?

No. Child custody and child support can be modified in the future. If there is a future modification of custody or support, the parent entitled to claim your child as a dependent could change. The best practice is to provide your former spouse a timely copy of Form 8332 signed by you for the appropriate tax year only.

14.16 Can my spouse and I split the child-care tax credit?

According to the Missouri child support guidelines, the value of the federal income tax credit for child care must be considered when determining the payor spouse's obligation to contribute to child-care expenses. The value of the federal child-care tax credit must be subtracted from the actual costs of child care to arrive at a figure for net child-care expenses owed by the spouse paying support.

Only the custodial parent is allowed to claim the credit. If you are a noncustodial parent and paying child care, you should talk to your lawyer about how to address this issue in your divorce decree.

14.17 Do I have to pay taxes on the portion of my spouse's 401(k) that was awarded to me in the divorce?

The division of these funds according to a qualified domestic relations order (QDRO) will prevent a tax upon the division of the funds. However, if you have been awarded a portion of your former spouse's 401(k) or 403(b) retirement plan, any distribution of these funds directly to you will be subject to regular income tax, plus a 10 percent penalty if you are not yet 59 ½. years of age. However, it may be possible for you to elect to receive all or a portion of these assets without incurring the 10 percent early withdrawal penalty (applicable if you are under age fifty-nine and one-half) under some circumstances. Talk with your attorney and your tax advisor to determine your options.

14.18 Is the cost of getting a divorce, including my attorney fees, tax deductible under any circumstances?

Your legal fees for getting a divorce are not deductible. However, a portion of your attorney fees may be deductible if they are for:

- The collection of sums included in your gross income, such as maintenance or interest income
- Advice regarding the determination of taxes or tax due

Attorney fees are "miscellaneous" deductions for individuals and are consequently limited to 2 percent of your adjusted gross income. More details can be found in IRS Publication 529 Miscellaneous Deductions.

You may also be able to deduct fees you pay to appraisers or accountants who help. Talk to your tax advisor about whether any portion of your attorney fees or other expenses from your divorce is deductible.

14.19 Do I have to complete a new Form W-4 for my employer because of my divorce?

Completing a new Form W-4, Employee's Withholding Certificate, will help you to claim the proper withholding allowances based upon your marital status and exemptions. If you neglect to complete a new W-4 to account for a spousal maintenance award, your tax withholdings may be off at the end of the year and result in unintended tax consequences. Also, if you are receiving spousal maintenance, you may need to make quarterly estimated tax payments. Consult with your tax advisor to ensure you are making the most preferable tax planning decision.

14.20 What is *innocent spouse relief* and how can it help me?

Innocent spouse relief refers to a method of obtaining relief from the Internal Revenue Service for taxes owed as a result of a joint income tax return filed during your marriage. Numerous factors affect your eligibility for innocent spouse tax relief, such as:

- You would suffer a financial hardship if you were required to pay the tax.

- You did not significantly benefit from the unpaid taxes.
- Your suffered abuse during your marriage.
- You thought your spouse would pay the taxes on the original return.

Talk with your attorney or your tax advisor if you are concerned about liability for taxes arising from joint tax returns filed during the marriage. You may benefit from a referral to an attorney who specializes in tax law.

15

Going to Court

For many clients, their divorce represents their first experience in the court system. Frequently, their expectations are based upon unrealistic and overly dramatic movie and television portrayals. However, it does not take too long to adjust these expectations after the first court appearance. The ever-present drama and "gotcha" moments that make television and movie depictions so engaging simply do not reflect the reality of the courtroom.

Going to court in connection with your divorce can mean many things, ranging from sitting in the courtroom while waiting for the lawyers and judges to conclude a conference, to testifying on the witness stand, and answering questions about your monthly living expenses.

Regardless of the nature of your court proceeding, going to court may elicit feelings of anxiety or even fear. Rest assured that these feelings of nervousness and uncertainty are normal. Understanding what will occur in court and being well prepared for any court hearings will help to relieve many of your concerns. Knowing the order of events, the role of the people in the courtroom, etiquette in the courtroom, and what is expected of you will make the entire experience easier. Your lawyer will be with you any time you go to court to answer your questions, and will provide guidance beforehand.

15.1 What do I need to know about appearing in court and court dates in general?

Court dates are important. Unless your attorney specifically tells you that you need not attend, plan on attending all court dates for which you receive notice. After receiving a notice from your attorney about a court date in your case, confirm whether your attendance will be required and put it on your calendar.

Ask your attorney about the nature of the hearing, including whether the judge will be receiving testimony of witnesses, reading affidavits, or merely listening to the arguments of the lawyers. Inquire about the anticipated length the hearing. It may be as short as a few minutes or as long as a day or more.

Ask whether it is necessary for you to meet with your attorney or take any other action to prepare for the hearing. If the hearing will be a testimonial motion, your attorney will want to meet with you in advance of the hearing to review and perhaps practice your direct examination and cross-examination. Your attorney may also need you to provide additional information or update the financial disclosures that you filed at the beginning of the case. Depending upon the type of hearing, your lawyer may ask you to arrive in advance of the scheduled hearing time to prepare.

In advance of any court dates you will be attending, determine a mutually agreeable time and place to meet your attorney. Make sure that you have your attorney's office number with you so that you can call his or her office to relay important information, such as if you will be late or need help finding the right courtroom. Sometimes lawyers have more than one meeting scheduled at the courthouse and can get tied up in a different courtroom. Maintaining an open line of communication with the attorney, or his or her office, will help avoid confusion.

Make sure you know the location of the courthouse, where to park, and the floor and room number of the courtroom. Planning for such simple matters as change for a parking meter can eliminate unnecessary stress. If you want someone to go to court with you to provide you support, check with your attorney first.

15.2 When and how often will I need to go to court?

When and how often you go to court will depend upon several factors. The level of conflict and animosity that exists in your case will likely be the most dominant factor. Highly contentious parties, who cannot agree on basic issues, will find themselves in front of the judge more frequently than parties who are able to resolve most issues themselves.

Although each judge handles his or her case load differently, many judges like to keep track of their cases by scheduling status conferences. Depending upon the complexity of your case, you may have only one conference or numerous conferences throughout the course of your divorce.

Only the attorneys attend some hearings, usually those on procedural matters. These matters frequently involve discovery disputes and requests for extensions of time or to shorten deadlines. These hearings are often brief and held in the judge's chambers rather than in the open courtroom. Other hearings, such as those for temporary custody and support, require live testimony and require the attendance of both parties and their attorneys.

If you and your spouse settle all of the issues in your case, although not required, you can choose to testify at a *non-contested hearing* in which the judge will review and approve your decree.

If your case proceeds to trial, your appearance will be required for the duration of the trial. In Missouri, divorce matters are heard before a judge only; juries do not hear divorces.

15.3 How much notice will I receive about appearing in court?

The amount of notice you will receive for any court hearing can vary from a few days to several weeks. In general, the Missouri Supreme Court Rules require that service of notice of hearing be made no later than five days before the date set for the hearing. However, in certain circumstances the trial court may shorten the amount of time. Ask your attorney whether and when it will be necessary for you to appear in court on your case so that you can make the necessary arrangements.

If you receive a notice of a hearing, contact your attorney immediately. He or she can tell you whether your appearance is required and what other steps are needed to prepare.

15.4   I am afraid to be alone in the same room with my spouse. When I go to court, is this going to happen if the lawyers go into the judge's office to discuss the case?

Prior to any court hearing, you and your spouse may be asked to wait while your attorneys meet with the judge to discuss preliminary matters. Let your lawyer know your concerns, and he or she can take the necessary steps to address the situation.

A number of options are likely available to ensure that you feel safe. These might include having you or your spouse wait in different locations or informing the court bailiff of the situation and having him or her keep an eye on the parties.

15.5   Do I have to go to court every time there is a court hearing on any motion?

Not necessarily. The judge will decide some matters after listening to the arguments of the lawyers. As mentioned, these hearings are frequently held in the judge's office, referred to as "chambers," and you will not be required to attend.

15.6   My spouse's lawyer keeps asking for *continuances of court dates*. Is there anything I can do to stop this?

It is not unusual for an attorney to request a *continuance* asking to reschedule a hearing or the entire trial. A party may request that a court date be postponed for many reasons, including a scheduling conflict, the lack of availability of one of the parties or an important witness, or the need for more time to prepare.

If your spouse's attorney repeatedly files for continuances, you should discuss your frustrations with your attorney and inquire what might be done to avoid future postponements. The trial judge does not automatically approve continuances. Your attorney will have the opportunity to object to any continuances requested by your spouse.

15.7   If I have to go to court, will I be put on the stand? Will there be a jury?

In Missouri, divorce matters are heard before a judge only; juries do not hear or decide divorces. Whether you will be put on the stand to testify will depend upon the nature of the hearing, the issues in dispute, the judge assigned to your case, and your attorney's strategy.

15.8 My lawyer said I need to be in court for our *PDL hearing* next week. What's going to happen?

A *PDL hearing* is held to determine such matters as temporary custody, child support, maintenance, and attorney's fees. PDL stands for *"pendente lite,"* a Latin phrase for temporary relief while the case is pending. There are also other issues, which may be addressed in a PDL hearing, including exclusive possession of the marital residence while your divorce is pending, and financial restraining orders.

The procedure for your temporary hearing can vary depending upon the county in which your case was filed and the judge to which the case is assigned

Most temporary hearings are testimonial hearings that require the party requesting temporary orders to testify and offer evidence to support his or her request. While these hearings are generally shorter than the final divorce trial, they can, in some cases, last for multiple days, depending upon the issues before the court.

In some counties, your hearing will be one of numerous other hearings on the judge's schedule for that day. You may find yourself in a courtroom with many other lawyers and their clients, all having matters scheduled before the court. If this is the case, you will likely have some waiting to do until the judge can address your matter. There is also the potential that the judge will not be able to reach your case for testimonial hearing that day and you will obtain a new date from the court.

15.9 Do I have to go to court if all of the issues in my case are settled?

It is up to the judge. If you and your spouse settle all of the issues in your case, most judges will allow you to submit an affidavit for judgment, which takes the place of you appearing to testify. However, the judge can require you and your spouse to appear to testify. Even if the judge does not require a "non-contested hearing" you may elect to have one. In a non-contested hearing, your attorney will have the opportunity

Going to Court.

to ask both you and your spouse questions relating to the agreements you and your spouse reached. At this hearing, the judge will review and approve your decree and may ask you questions as well.

15.10 Are there any rules about courtroom etiquette that I need to know?

Knowing a few tips about being in the courtroom will make your experience easier.

- Dress appropriately. Avoid overly casual dress, lots of jewelry, revealing clothing, and extreme hairstyles.
- Do not take beverages into the courtroom. Most courts have rules that do not allow food and drink in courtrooms. If you need water, ask your lawyer.
- Dispose of chewing gum before giving testimony.
- Do not talk aloud in the courtroom unless you're on the witness stand or being questioned by the judge.
- Sit where your attorney tells you to sit. Do not enter the area designated for the attorneys and do not use the doors utilized by the judge to enter and exit the courtroom.
- Stand up whenever the judge is entering or leaving the courtroom.
- Remember to turn off your electronic devices including cell phones.
- Be mindful that the judge may be observing you and those you bring to the hearing at all times.
- Do not display extreme reactions or make outbursts during another witnesses' testimony.

Although you may feel anxious initially, you'll likely feel more relaxed about the courtroom setting once your hearing gets underway.

15.11 What is the role of the *bailiff*?

The *bailiff* provides support for the judge and lawyers in the management of the court calendar and the courtroom. He or she assists provides security within the courtroom and may assist the judge with other functions such as managing the case load and obtaining copies of orders.

15.12 Will there be a *court reporter,* and what will he or she do?

A *court reporter* is a professional trained to make an accurate record of the words spoken and manage documents offered into evidence during court proceedings. Some courtrooms use tape recording devices rather than court reporters.

A written transcript of a court proceeding may be purchased from the court reporter. If your case is appealed, the court of appeals will use the transcript prepared by the court reporter to review the facts of your case.

Some hearings are held "off the record," which means that the court reporter is not making a record of what is being said. Ordinarily these are matters for which no appeal is expected.

15.13 Will I be able to talk to my attorney while we are in court?

During court proceedings it is important that your attorney give his or her attention to anything being said by the judge, witnesses, or your spouse's lawyer. For this reason, your attorney will avoid talking with you when anyone else in the courtroom is speaking.

Plan to have pen and paper with you when you go to court. If your court proceeding is underway and your lawyer is listening to what is being said by others in the courtroom, write him or her a note with your questions or comments.

It is critical that your attorney hear each question asked by the other lawyer and all answers given by each witness. If not, opportunities for making objections to inappropriate evidence may be lost. If the court hearing is lengthy, breaks will be taken. You can use this time to discuss with your attorney any questions or observations you have about the proceeding.

15.14 What questions might my lawyer ask me at about the problems in our marriage and why I want the divorce?

Because the conduct of the parties can potentially impact both the division of property and spousal maintenance under Missouri law, you should expect your attorney to ask questions about the conduct of your spouse that contributed to the irretrievable breakdown of the marriage.

The questions may be similar to these:

Attorney: During the course of your marriage, has your spouse engaged in any conduct that placed a burden on the marriage?

You: Yes.

Attorney: Please tell the court the nature of that conduct?

You: My husband has had a gambling problem for many years.

Attorney: How has your husband's gambling problem impacted your marriage?

You: It has been a near daily source of argument between us and has impacted us financially. We have had to cancel trips due to excessive losses and on several occasions we have not been able to pay our monthly bills.

Attorney: Are you asking the court to take your husband's gambling into consideration when dividing what remains of the marital property?

You: Yes.

It will be up to the judge to decide whether the conduct of you or your spouse has any effect on the divorce judgment.

15.15 My lawyer said that the judge has issued a *pretrial order* having to do with my upcoming trial and that we'll have to comply with it. What does this mean?

Some judges will enter *pretrial orders* that require that certain tasks be accomplished in accordance with established deadlines prior to trial. Pretrial orders help to keep the case on track for trial and serve to ensure that the attorneys have exchanged necessary information according to a specified schedule. A typical pretrial order might include:

- A deadline for designating expert witnesses
- A deadline for the completion of discovery
- Dates for the exchange of trial exhibits
- Dates for updating financial affidavits
- A requirement that the attorneys submit a list of issues that have been settled or those that remain in dispute

Ask your lawyer for a copy of the pretrial order.

15.16 What is a *pretrial conference?*

A *pretrial conference* is a meeting held with the lawyers and the judge to review information related to an upcoming trial, such as:

- How long the trial is expected to last
- The issues in dispute
- The law surrounding the disputed issues
- The identification of witnesses
- Trial exhibits
- The status of negotiations

If a pretrial conference is held in your case, ask your attorney whether you should attend. Your attorney may request that you either be present for the conference or be available by phone.

15.17 Besides meeting with my lawyer, is there anything else I should do to prepare for my upcoming trial?

Yes. Be sure to review your deposition and any information you provided in your discovery, such as answers to interrogatories. It is possible that at trial you will be asked some of the same questions. It is important to remain consistent, however if you think you might give different answers at trial, you should discuss the best way to do so with your lawyer. Also be sure to review your financial affidavits (Statement of Property/Statement of Income and Expense) to make sure that they remain accurate.

15.18 I'm meeting with my lawyer to prepare for trial. How do I make the most of these meetings?

Meeting with your lawyer to prepare for your trial is an important step towards achieving a good outcome. Come to the meeting prepared to discuss the following:

- The issues in your case
- Your desired outcome on each of the issues
- The questions you might be asked at trial by your attorney on direct examination

- The questions you might be asked at trial by your spouse's attorney on cross-examination
- The exhibits that will be offered into evidence during the trial
- The witnesses for your trial
- The status of negotiations

Your meeting with your lawyer will help you better understand what to expect at your trial and make the trial experience easier.

15.19 My lawyer says that the law firm is busy with trial preparation. What exactly is my lawyer doing to prepare for my trial?

A multitude tasks are necessary to properly prepare your case for trial. These are just some of them:

- Developing and refining arguments to be made on each of the contested issues
- Researching and reviewing the relevant law in your case
- Reviewing the facts of your case to determine which witnesses are best suited to testifying about them
- Reviewing, selecting, and preparing exhibits
- Preparing outlines for examination of all witnesses
- Preparing an opening/closing statement
- Reviewing rules on evidence to prepare for anticipated objections at trial
- Determining the order of witnesses and all exhibits
- Drafting motions to be presented and argued prior to the commencement of trial
- Preparing your file for the day in court, including preparing a trial notebook with essential information

A trial is a complex and carefully orchestrated presentation. All of the tasks listed above are important preparations that will aid your lawyer in achieving the best possible outcome for you in your divorce. He or she will be engaged in many important actions to fully prepare your case for trial.

15.20 How do I know who my witnesses will be at trial?

Well in advance of your trial date, your lawyer will discuss with you whether witnesses, other than you and your spouse, will be necessary. Potential witnesses might include family members, friends, child-care providers, accountants, or any other person with important information concerning your case. When thinking of potential witnesses, consider your relationship with the witness, whether that witness has had an opportunity to observe relevant facts, and whether the witness has knowledge different from that of other witnesses. For more information on identifying potential witnesses, please see question 8.18 in chapter 8.

You may also have one or more expert witnesses testify on your behalf. An expert witness will provide opinion testimony based upon specialized knowledge, training, or experience. For example, a psychologist, real estate appraiser, or accountant may provide expert testimony on your behalf.

15.21 My divorce is scheduled for trial. Does this mean there is no hope for a settlement?

Many cases are settled after a trial date is set. Obtaining a trial setting frequently causes divorcing spouses to think about both the risks and costs of going to trial. These realities can help you and your spouse focus on what is most important to you and lead you toward a negotiated settlement. Given the high cost of trial preparation, it makes the best financial sense to engage in settlement negotiations well in advance of your trial date. However, it is not uncommon for cases to settle a few days before trial, or even at the courthouse before your trial begins.

15.22 Can I prevent my spouse or others from being in the courtroom?

No. Your spouse has a legal interest in the outcome of the divorce, and he or she has a right to be present. Unless the case is sealed, your courtroom will, most likely, be open to the public. Consequently, it is not uncommon for persons not involved in your divorce to pass through the courtroom at various times simply because they have other business with the court.

15.23 Can I take a friend or family member with me to court?

Most likely, yes. If you intend to take anyone to court with you let your attorney know in advance. Make sure to choose someone who is able to focus attention on supporting you rather than on his or her own personal feelings concerning your divorce.

15.24 Can my friends and family be present in the courtroom during my trial?

It depends upon whether they will be witnesses in your case. In most cases, in which witnesses are testifying, the attorneys request that the court exclude the other witnesses from the courtroom. The purpose for the exclusion is to prevent the testimony of the potential witness from being influenced by the things they would hear from other witnesses.

Once a witness has completed his or her testimony, he or she will ordinarily be allowed to remain in the courtroom for the remainder of the trial.

15.25 I want to do a good job testifying as a witness in my divorce trial. What are some tips?

In order to be an effective, credible witness, keep the following principles in mind:

- Tell the truth. Although this may not be always be comfortable, it is critical if you want the judge to believe your testimony.
- Listen carefully to the complete question before answering. If you do not understand the question ask the attorney to repeat or rephrase.
- Take the time you need to consider your answer before responding. You may be asked some questions that call for a thoughtful response. If you need a moment to reflect on an answer before you give it, allow yourself that time.
- Slow down. It's easy to speed up our speech when we are anxious. Taking your time with your answers ensures that the judge hears you and that the court reporter can accurately record your testimony.

- If you do not know the answer to a specific question do not speculate. It is not detrimental to say that you do not know.
- If the question calls for a "yes" or "no" answer, provide a "yes" or "no" answer. Then wait for the attorney to ask you the next question. If there is more you want to explain, remember that you have already told your attorney all the important facts and he or she will make sure you allowed to give any testimony significant in your case.
- Don't argue with the judge or the lawyers.
- Stop speaking if an objection is made by one of the lawyers. Wait until the judge has decided whether to allow you to answer.

15.26 Should I be worried about being cross-examined by my spouse's lawyer at trial?

You should be prepared, not worried. Prior to trial, you will want to meet with your lawyer to discuss what to expect on cross-examination and how to handle the questions that you'll be asked. You should know the major issues that will be addressed at trial, as they will mostly likely have been broached at some point during discovery.

Every case has both positives and negatives. Practice your responses to the negative aspects of your case by having your attorney ask you questions concerning these topics as if he were your spouse's attorney. After you have completed the exercise you can discuss with your attorney if there are better or more effective ways of responding to the difficult questions.

Above all else, do not lose your composure. Try not to take the questions personally; remember that the lawyer is fulfilling a duty to advocate for your spouse's interests. If you do lose your cool, you run the risk of the judge forming negative conclusions about you. Remember that you are just doing your best to tell the truth about the facts.

15.27 What happens on the day of trial?

Although no two trials are the same, the following steps will occur in most divorce trials:

- The attorneys meet with the judge in chambers or open court to discuss procedural issues, such as pretrial motions, the status of settlement discussions, the presentation of witnesses, and when breaks might be taken.
- The judge, on the record, will address all preliminary matters including pretrial motions.
- The parties will file requests for findings of fact and conclusions of law with the court.
- If the court permits, both attorneys will be given the opportunity to make opening statements.
- The attorney for the petitioner will calls witnesses to testify on behalf of the petitioner.
- The attorney for the respondent will be given the opportunity to cross-examine all of petitioner's witnesses.
- The attorney for the respondent will calls witnesses to testify on behalf of the respondent.
- The attorney for the petitioner will be given the opportunity to cross-examine all of respondent's witnesses.
- The petitioner's lawyer calls any *rebuttal witnesses,* that is, witnesses whose testimony contradicts the testimony of the respondent's witnesses.
- If the court permits, both attorneys will be given the opportunity to make closing arguments.

15.28 Will the judge decide my case the day I go to court?

Not likely. Typically there is so much information from the trial for the judge to consider that it is not possible for the judge to give an immediate ruling. There are also several issues, such as custody, that require the judge to make specific written findings that cannot be accomplished quickly. The judge will likely want to review documents, review the law, perform calculations, review his or her notes, and give thoughtful consideration to the issues to be decided. For this reason, it may be weeks or months before a ruling is made.

When a judge does not make a ruling immediately upon the conclusion of a trial, it is said that the case has been "taken under advisement."

16

The Appeals Process

Almost no one gets exactly what he or she asked for at trial. Typically, both sides are pleased with some portions of their judgment of dissolution of marriage and displeased with others. If you believe that the trial court did not reach the correct result on one or more issues in your case, you have the ability to appeal the judgment. Appellate courts operate very differently from trial courts. They do not take new evidence, hear witnesses, or interact with the litigants. Rather, they determine the correctness of the trial court result based upon the written briefs and oral arguments of the parties' attorneys. In making their determinations, the courts of appeal look to the record on appeal, which includes a transcript of the trial testimony, selected trial exhibits, and relevant pleadings from the trial court's file. As such, the appellate courts are constrained by what occurred at the trial level.

Shortly after you receive the judgment, you should meet with your attorney to discuss the terms of the judgment as well as your next steps to address any problem areas contained in the judgment. The Missouri Supreme Court Rules give the trial court a period of thirty days after the judgment has been entered to modify, amend, or vacate its judgment. Also during this thirty-day period, both parties have the ability to file posttrial motions to request, among other things, an amendment to the judgment or even a new trial. The filing of an authorized posttrial motion extends the time during which the trial court retains control over its judgment from thirty days to ninety days after filing the motion, unless the court makes an earlier ruling.

Your attorney may be able to persuade the trial judge to alter the judgment in your favor through a posttrial motion. If, after all of your remedies at the trial level have been exhausted and the judgment remains unacceptable, you should discuss with your attorney the feasibility of an appeal.

16.1 How much time after my divorce do I have to file an appeal?

For the Court of Appeals to consider your appeal timely, you must file a notice of appeal with the trial court no later than ten days following the date that the judgment becomes final. If neither party files any authorized posttrial motions, the judgment becomes final thirty days after the date the trial court enters the judgment. If either party files an authorized posttrial motion, the date that judgment becomes final varies according the specific circumstances of the case.

Although Missouri law contains provisions that permit, under certain circumstances, parties to file appeals after the deadlines have passed, you would be best served to preserve your right to appeal in a timely manner. Failure to comply with the deadlines may preclude your appeal from ever being heard. Discuss this with your attorney, sooner rather than later.

16.2 Can I appeal a temporary order?

As a general rule, parties can only appeal final judgments. However, Missouri treats awards according to the Missouri statutes governing temporary (PDL) orders as well as attorney fee awards as final, appealable judgments even though the underlying divorce case remains pending. Additionally, a party can appeal a judgment that resolves one or more, but not all claims that exist in a case so long as the judgment provides that "there is no just reason for delay."

16.3 What parts of the decree can be appealed?

You have the right to appeal any portion of the decree you deem appropriate. Keep in mind that before you appeal issues relating to the form or language of the judgment, including the trial court's failure to make required findings, you must first give the trial court the opportunity to address these issues in

The Appeals Process

a motion to amend the judgment. If you fail to do so, you will not preserve the issue at the appellate level.

16.4   Will my attorney recommend I appeal specific aspects of the decree, or will I have to request it?

After reviewing the judgment you should make a list of the specific aspects of the judgment you would like to have addressed on appeal and discuss those issues with your attorney. Both the decision to appeal, as well as the determination of which issues to appeal, should be made with your attorney and may be based upon many considerations. Your attorney will be able to give you an opinion, based upon his or her knowledge of the evidence presented at trial, as to whether some or all of your issues merit an appeal.

The attorney that you have handle the appeal may not be the attorney that represented you at trial. Some trial attorneys simply do not handle appellate work. Also, not infrequently, parties elect to retain different counsel for the purpose of appeal. If you do elect to retain different counsel to pursue an appeal on your behalf, it is important your trial attorney and your appellate attorney coordinate with one another to timely file the documents that are necessary preserve your right to appeal.

16.5   Under what circumstances should an appeal be filed?

The appellate process can be both long and expensive. The decision to pursue an appeal should not be made without careful consideration of the potential outcomes and likelihood of success, and the economic cost in relation to any potential relief sought. If you remain uncertain whether to pursue an appeal, you should consider filing a timely notice of appeal for the sole purpose of preserving your right to do so. Such action will allow you to avoid the obstacles associated with filing a late notice of appeal if you ultimately decide to proceed. If after filing your notice of appeal, you elect not to move forward, you can simply dismiss the appeal.

Each case will have its own unique set of issues. There are many factors you will want to take into consideration and address with your attorney before filing. These factors include, but are not limited to:

- Whether the judge had the legal authority to make the decisions set forth in your decree
- Whether your legal position on appeal asks the appellate court to change already established precedent
- The standard of review that the appellate court will apply to the specific issues raised by your appeal
- The number of unique issues that will be addressed in the appeal and the cost associated therewith.
- The likelihood that your appeal will result in a cross appeal or motion for attorney's fees by your former spouse
- The length of time an appeal can be expected to take
- The requirement for posting a bond to prevent collection on any money judgments during the pendency of the appeal
- Your attorney's opinion regarding the likelihood of the success of your appeal

16.6   Are there any disadvantages to filing an appeal?

As with any decision to pursue an avenue with an uncertain outcome, there are potential disadvantages. The potential exists for you to spend significant money on the appeal only to end up with the exact same or perhaps even less favorable results.

16.7   Is an attorney necessary to appeal?

Although no law prohibits you from representing yourself in the court of appeals, the technicalities associated with the appeals process, including very detailed and specific brief drafting rules, almost invariably proves impossible for most people to handle on their own. Given the complex nature of the appellate process, you should have an attorney if you intend to file an appeal.

16.8   How long does the appeals process usually take?

It depends. An appeal can take anywhere from several months to well over a year. An appeal may also result in the appellate court requiring further proceedings by the trial court.

16.9 What are the steps in the appeals process?

There are many steps which your lawyer will take on your behalf in the appeal process, including:

- Identifying the issues to be appealed
- Filing a notice of appeal
- Obtaining the necessary court documents and trial exhibits (the "legal file") to submit to the appellate court
- Obtaining an official trial transcript (the transcribed copy of everything that was on the record at the trial, including testimony by witnesses, statements by the judge, statements of the lawyers). The transcript is prepared from either the transcription of court reporter that was present at the trial or the recording that was made at the trial.
- Performing legal research to support your arguments on appeal
- Preparing and filing a document known as a *brief,* which sets for the facts of the case and relevant law, complete with citations to court transcript, court documents, and prior cases
- Making an oral argument before the judges of the appellate court

16.10 Is filing and pursuing an appeal expensive?

The appellate process can be an expensive one. In addition to filing fees and legal fees, there is likely to be a substantial cost for the preparation of the transcript of the trial testimony and the legal file.

16.11 If I do not file an appeal, can I ever go back to court to change my decree?

As long as your children remain unemancipated, the trial court will always retain jurisdiction to modify child custody and child support. Similarly, if a divorce decree contains an award of modifiable spousal maintenance, the trial court will have the authority to modify the original award. However, other aspects of a decree are not modifiable, such as the division of property and debts or the award of attorney fees.

In Closing

We hope the questions and answers in this book have been helpful to you. Take heart in knowing that, if you do find yourself in the middle of a divorce, you will have plenty of time to consider all options before making important decisions. In almost all cases, it is highly unlikely that you will ever be called upon to make a decision on the spur of the moment about any aspect of your divorce. You should rely heavily upon your lawyer for advice and guidance about any topics, and remember, your case is different from any others.

Just as no two individuals are exactly alike, no two divorce cases are exactly alike. It is difficult to list every reason you may find your divorce is so disorienting and emotionally difficult. Such a list would certainly be a lengthy one. However, many clients have told us over the years that among the worst aspects of divorce is that their "lives are in limbo" while their divorce cases is pending. Another troublesome aspect of divorce is being in an adversarial relationship with your former spouse—the one individual who knows almost everything there is to know about you and your life.

Nevertheless, the divorce process is a temporary one and it will end. The process will be more bearable if you always keep your eyes on the "big picture" and not on the immediate aggravations of the day. Focus on getting through the process with the objective of returning to a full life. Such an attitude will provide you with the strength necessary to navigate this new and unfamiliar course. We wish you every good wish as you do so.

Appendix

Sample Petition for Divorce

IN THE CIRCUIT COURT OF THE COUNTY OF _____
STATE OF MISSOURI

In Re the Marriage of:)
)
_____,   )
)   Cause No.
            Petitioner,   )
)
vs.   )   Division No.
)
_____,   )
)
            Respondent.   )

PETITION FOR DISSOLUTION OF MARRIAGE

COMES NOW Petitioner, _____, and for his Petition for Dissolution of Marriage, states:

1. Petitioner is currently a resident of _____ County, Missouri and has been for more than ninety (90) days immediately preceding the filing of the Petition. Petitioner's Social Security Number is ***-**-XXXX, and he presently resides at _____ _____. Petitioner is presently employed by _____.

2. Respondent is and has been a resident of Missouri for more than ninety (90) days immediately preceding the filing of the Petition.

Sample Petition for Divorce (Continued)

Respondent's Social Security Number is ***-**-XXXX, and she presently resides at _____.
Respondent is presently employed by _____
_____.

3. Petitioner and Respondent were married on
_____, and the marriage is
registered in _____ County, in the State of
_____.

4. Respondent and Petitioner were separated on
_____.

5. There are no unemancipated children born of the marriage.

6. Upon information and belief, Respondent is not now pregnant.

7. Neither Petitioner nor Respondent are members of the Armed Forces of the United States.

8. The parties are possessed of marital property to be divided by the court and Petitioner is possessed of separate/non-marital property.

9. There is no reasonable likelihood that the marriage of the parties can be preserved and, therefore, the marriage is irretrievably broken.

10. Petitioner is without sufficient funds to pay attorney's fees, Court costs and expenses herein.

11. Respondent is able-bodied and is gainfully employed, earning a sum sufficient to enable Respondent to provide for the maintenance of the Petitioner, and to provide Petitioner with such sums of money as will enable Petitioner to employ counsel to represent Petitioner in the prosecution of this action and to provide suit monies and to pay the costs herein.

WHEREFORE, Petitioner prays that the Court to enter its judgment dissolving the parties' marriage; setting aside Petitioner's separate/non-marital property to him; dividing the parties' marital property and debts in an equitable manner; awarding Petitioner a reasonable sum for his maintenance; awarding Petitioner his attorney's fees and the costs of this proceeding; and for such other and further relief as the Court deems just and proper in the circumstances.

_____
PETITIONER

STATE OF MISSOURI   )
)   ss
COUNTY OF _____   )

_____, being first duly sworn, upon his oath, states that he is the Petitioner in the above-styled cause, that he has

Sample Petition for Divorce (Continued)

read the foregoing Petition for Dissolution of Marriage and that the statements contained therein are true and correct according to his best knowledge, information and belief.

Subscribed and sworn to before me, a Notary Public, this _____ day of _____, _____.

_____
Notary Public

My commission expires:

Sample Letter to Spouse

Mr. John Doe
1234 Lane
St. Louis, Missouri 63105

     In re: Jane and John Doe

Dear Mr. Doe:

I have been retained by Jane Doe to represent her in her Petition for Dissolution of Marriage against you. Mrs. Doe has requested that we not have you formally served at this point in time. In accordance with her wishes, we are sending you all of the relevant materials that you would have otherwise been served with, in this letter. These materials are:

1. Civil Summons
2. Family Tracking Sheet
3. Case Filing Information Sheet
4. Petitioner's Petition for Dissolution of Marriage
5. Petitioner's Statement of Income & Expense
6. Petitioner's Statement of Property
7. Automatic Family Court Order Rule 68.3
8. Mandatory Exchange of Documents Rule 68.5

If you will be retaining an attorney to represent your interests, I would ask that you forward these materials to him/her at your earliest opportunity. If you will not be retaining the services of an attorney I would respectfully request that you execute the enclosed Entry of Appearance and Waiver of Service of Process form in front of a notary public and file this document at

Sample Letter to Spouse (Continued)

the _____ County Courthouse in _____. If you do not wish to do so, it will be necessary for us to have a process server formally serve you with the aforementioned documents, in order to proceed with the case.

If you will not be retaining the services of an attorney I would ask that you please also fill out and file the attached blank Statement of Property and Statement of Income and Expense.

Please be advised that we represent Mrs. Doe only. We do not represent you and cannot provide you with any legal advice. If you have any questions, please contact an attorney of your choosing.

Sincerely,

_____, Attorney at Law

Enclosures
Cc: Mrs. Jane Doe

Sample Voluntary Court Appearance Document

IN THE FAMILY COURT OF THE COUNTY OF ST. LOUIS
STATE OF MISSOURI

In re the Marriage of:	)	
Jane Doe, SS# XXX-XX-1234	)	
Petitioner,	)	Cause No.
and	)	Division No.
John Doe SS# XXX-XX-4321	)	
Respondent.	)	

ENTRY OF APPEARANCE
AND WAIVER OF SERVICE OF SUMMONS

COMES NOW Respondent, John Doe, and voluntarily enters his appearance, *pro se,* in the above referenced matter. Respondent acknowledges receipt of a copy of Petitioner's Petition for Dissolution of Marriage,

Appendix

Sample Voluntary Court Appearance Document (Continued)

Petitioner's Statement of Income and Expenses and Petitioner's Statement of Property. Respondent specifically waives the necessity for personal service of Summons and copies of the Petitioner's Petition for Dissolution of Marriage, Petitioner's Statement of Income and Expenses and Petitioner's Statement of Property upon him. Respondent also affirmatively states that he is over the age of eighteen (18) years, and he is not a member of the Armed Forces nor on active duty.

_____
John Doe, Respondent

STATE OF MISSOURI　　　　)
　　　　　　　　　　　　　)　　SS.
COUNTY OF ST. LOUIS　　　)

　　　　Comes now, John Doe, of lawful age and being first duly sworn upon his oath, states that he is the Respondent named in the above and foregoing document, that he has read same and that the statements contained therein are true and correct to the best of his knowledge, information and belief, and he has signed same as his free act and deed.

　　　　SUBSCRIBED and SWORN to before me this _____day of _____, 20___.

_____
Notary Public

My Commission Expires:

Resources

Annual Credit Report Request Service
P.O. Box 105283
Atlanta, GA 30348-5283
Phone: (877) 322–8228
www.annualcreditreport.com

Internal Revenue Service (IRS)
www.irs.gov
Phone: (800) 829-1040 tax assistance for individual tax questions
or (800) 829-4933 for business tax questions.

Legal Aid of Western Missouri
1125 Grand Boulevard, Suite 1900
Kansas City, MO 64106
Phone: (816) 474-6750
www.lawmo.org

Legal Services of Eastern Missouri
4232 Forest Park Avenue
St. Louis, MO 63108
Phone: (314) 534-4200 or toll-free (800) 444-0514
www.lsem.org

Legal Services of Southern Missouri
809 North Campbell Avenue
Springfield, MO 65802
Phone: (417) 881-0533 or toll-fee (800) 444-4863
www.lsosm.org

Mid-Missouri Legal Services (Columbia Office)
1201 West Broadway
Columbia, MO 65203
Phone: (573) 442-0116 or toll-free (800) 568-4931
www.mmls.org

Mid-Missouri Legal Services (Jefferson City Office)
428 East Capitol Avenue, Suite 200
Jefferson City, MO 65101
Phone: (573) 634-4545 or toll-free (888) 476-4545
www.mmls.org

Missouri Courts
www.courts.mo.gov/casenet/base/welcome.do

**Missouri Department of Social Services
(Family Support Division)**
https://dss.mo.gov/fsd/
The location of local offices throughout the state can be found on the website.

Missouri Family Support Payment Center
PO Box 6790
Jefferson City MO 65102-6790
Phone: (800) 859-7999
https://mo.smartchildsupport.com

Saint Louis University Children and Youth Advocacy Clinic
http://law.slu.edu/academics/clinics/civil-advocacy-clinics

Social Security Administration
Office of Public Inquiries
Windsor Park Building
6401 Security Boulevard
Baltimore, MD 21235
Phone: (800) 772-1213
www.ssa.gov

**University of Missouri
Kansas City Child and Family Services Clinic**
https://law.umkc.edu/academics/clinical-programs/child-and-family-services-clinic
Phone: (816) 235-6336

Washington University
Children and Family Advocacy Clinic
http://law.wustl.edu/clinicaled/pages.aspx?id=6829

Glossary

Affidavit: A written statement of facts made under oath and signed before a notary public. Affidavits are used primarily when there will not be a hearing in open court with live testimony. The attorney will prepare an affidavit to present relevant facts. The person signing the affidavit may be referred to as the *affiant*.

Allegation: A statement that one party claims is true.

Answer: A written response to the petition for divorce. It serves to admit or deny the allegations in the petition and may also make claims against the opposing party. This is sometimes called a *responsive pleading*. An answer should be filed within thirty days of either (a) the complaint being served or (b) the defendant's voluntary appearance being filed with the court.

Appeal: The process by which a higher court reviews the decision of a lower court. In Missouri family law cases, a person will first file an appeal with the Missouri Court of Appeals. After that appeal is decided there may be a further appeal to the Missouri Supreme Court.

Application for relocation: A parent's written request to the court seeking permission to relocate with the children.

Child support: Financial support for a child paid by the one parent to the other parent.

Contempt of court: The willful and intentional failure of a party to comply with a judgment. Contempt may be punishable by fines or incarceration.

Contested case: Any case in which the parties cannot reach an agreement. A contested case will result in a trial to have the judge decide disputed issues.

Court order: A court-issued document setting forth the judge's orders. An order can be issued based upon the parties' agreement or the judge's decision. An order may require the parties to perform certain acts or set forth their rights and responsibilities. An order is put in writing, signed by the judge, and filed with the court.

Cross-examination: The questioning of a witness by the opposing counsel during trial or at a deposition, in response to questions asked by the other lawyer.

Custody: The legal right and responsibility awarded by a court for the possession of, care of, and decision-making for a minor child.

Decree of dissolution: A final court order dissolving the marriage, dividing property and debts, ordering support, and entering other orders regarding finances and the minor children.

Deposition: A witness's testimony taken out of court, under oath, and in the presence of lawyers and a court reporter. If a person gives a different testimony at the time of trial, he or she can be impeached with the deposition testimony; that is, statements made at a deposition can be used to show untruthfulness if a different answer is given at trial.

Direct examination: The initial questioning of a witness in court by the lawyer who called him or her to the stand.

Discovery: A process used by attorneys to discover information from the opposing party for the purpose of fully assessing a case for settlement or trial. Types of discovery include interrogatories, requests for production of documents, and requests for admissions.

Dissolution: The act of terminating or dissolving a marriage.

Equitable distribution of property: The method by which real and personal property and debts are divided in a divorce. Given all economic circumstances of the parties, Missouri law requires that marital property and debts be divided in an equitable manner.

Ex parte: Usually in reference to a motion, the term used to describe an appearance of only one party before the judge, without other party being present. For example, an *ex parte* restraining order may be granted immediately after the filing of a complaint for divorce.

Glossary

Guardian *ad litem* (GAL): A licensed attorney appointed by court to represent the minor children and make recommendations to the court regarding custody.

Hearing: Any proceeding before the court for the purpose of resolving disputed issues between the parties through presentation of testimony, affidavits, exhibits, or argument.

Hold-harmless clause: A term in a court order that requires one party to assume responsibility for a debt and to protect the other spouse from any loss or expense in connection with it, as in to hold harmless from liability.

Interrogatories: Written questions sent from one party to the other that are used to obtain facts or opinions related to the divorce.

Joint custody: The shared right and responsibility of both parents awarded by the court for possession, care, and decision-making for children.

Maintenance: Court-ordered spousal support payments from one party to another, often to enable the recipient spouse to become economically independent.

Mediation: A process by which a neutral third party facilitates negotiations between the parties on a wide range of issues.

Motion: A written application to the court for relief, such as temporary child support, custody, or restraining orders.

Motion to modify: A party's written pleading to the court to change a prior order regarding custody, child support, maintenance or any other order that the court may change by law.

No-fault divorce: The type of divorce that does not require evidence of marital misconduct. This means that abandonment, cruelty, and adultery are neither relevant nor required to be proven for the purposes of granting the divorce.

Notice of hearing: A written statement sent to the opposing lawyer or spouse listing the date and place of a hearing and the nature of the matters that will be heard by the court. In Missouri, one party is required to give the other party reasonable notice of any court hearing.

Party: The person in a legal action whose rights or interests will be affected by the divorce. For example, in a divorce the parties include the wife and husband.

Pending: During the case. For example, the judge may award you temporary support while your case is pending.

Petition: The first document filed with the clerk of the court in an action for divorce, legal separation, or paternity. The petition sets forth the facts on which the requested relief is based.

Petitioner: The person who files the petition initiating a divorce.

Pleadings: Documents filed with the court.

Qualified domestic relations order (QDRO): A type of court order that provides for direct payment from a retirement account to a former spouse.

Qualified medical support order (QMSO): A type of court order that provides a former spouse certain rights regarding medical insurance and information.

Request for production of documents: A written request for documents sent from one party to the other during the discovery process.

Respondent: The responding party to a divorce; the party who did not file the complaint initiating the divorce.

Sequester: To order prospective witnesses out of the courtroom until they have concluded giving their testimony.

Setoff: A debt or financial obligation of one spouse that is deducted from the debt or financial obligation of the other spouse.

Settlement: The agreed resolution of disputed issues.

Show cause: Written application to the court to hold another person in contempt of court for violating or failing to comply with a current court order.

Stipulation: An agreement reached between parties or an agreement by their attorneys.

Subpoena: A document delivered to a person or witness that requires him or her to appear in court, appear for a deposition, or produce documents. Failure to comply could result in punishment by the court. A subpoena requesting documents is called a *subpoena duces tecum.*

Temporary restraining order (TRO): An order of the court prohibiting a party from certain behavior. For example, a temporary restraining order may order a person not to transfer any funds during a pending divorce action.

Trial: A formal court hearing in which the judge will decide disputed issues raised by the parties' pleadings.

Under advisement: A term used to describe the status of a case, usually after a court hearing on a motion or a trial, when the judge has not yet made a decision.

Index

Index

239

Index

Index

245

Index

room with, 29
steps of, 91
sexual orientation, 114–115
shame, 28
shared parenting, 119–120
short sale, 159
significant other, 154
Social Security, 182
Social Security disability
  benefits (SSD), 138
sole legal custody, 103
sole physical custody, 118–
  119, 128
sources of all income, 137–
  139
speaking ill of spouse, 28
sperm, 173
split custody, 122
split physical custody, 104
spousal maintenance, 147, *see
  also* maintenance
spousal support, *see* alimony;
  maintenance
spouse
  abuse by, 84–85
  amicable divorce with, 18
  anger towards, 29
  arguing with, 127
  attorney fees, role in pay-
    ing, 63
  communicating with, 127
  complaint by, 12
  consent for divorce by, 7–8
  court, attendance in, 203,
    210
  Disneyland parent behavior
    of, 24–25
  fearing your (*see*
    emergencies)
  fighting with, 127
  financial information
    provided by, 17–18
  health insurance for,
    through employer, 177
  infidelity by, 5–6
  letter to, 225–226
  locating, 8–9
  loving feelings towards, 27

maintenance, income and
  amount of, 150, 152
serving papers to, 11–12
settlement conference,
  sitting in same room with,
    29
speaking ill of, 28
taxes, proving income for,
  150–151
temporary court order
  requested by, 14
statement of account, 52–53
status for filing taxes, 194–
  195
status quo, 185
stocks, 168, 171
stress
  counseling for coping with,
    26–27
  divorce process, coping
    with, 21–31
  lowering, 84
student loans, 186
subpoena, 1, 69–70
summer vacation, 140
supervised parenting time,
  124–125, *see also* parenting
  time; visitation
supervised visitation, 125
Supreme Court, 41, 123, 136,
  215

T

talking about divorce with
  child/children, 23–24
taxes, 191–199
  on alimony, 192–194
  capital gains, 196
  child-care credit for, 197
  on child support, 192
  dependents for, 196
  documents need for
    preparing, 195
  exemptions for, 197
  fees for divorce and, 198
  house, consequences of
    selling, 195–196
  income, 191–192
  innocent spouse relief and,

About the Authors

Cary J. Mogerman, Esq., is the managing member of Zerman Mogerman, LLC in St. Louis, Missouri. He obtained his juris doctorate degree from the Washington University School of Law and his bachelor of arts degree from Drake University. He is a Fellow of the American Academy of Matrimonial Lawyers and a Diplomate of the American College of Family Trial Lawyers, an organization limited to 100 lawyers throughout the nation. He has been recognized in Woodard/White's The Best Lawyers in America, for Family Law, since 1999.

Mogerman is a past recipient of the "Roger P. Krumm Family Law Practitioner of the Year" award from the Missouri Bar Family Law Section. He has been recognized as a Missouri/Kansas "Super Lawyer" since 2005, a "Missouri/Kansas Top 100 Super Lawyer," and a "St. Louis Top 50 Super Lawyer" by the same publication since 2006. For ten years, Mr. Mogerman has served on the faculty of the AAML Institute for Family Law Associates, offered annually in Chicago, Illinois, and since 2012, he has been a member of the national faculty of the annual Family Law Trial Advocacy Institute, offered for eight days every summer in Boulder, Colorado by the American Bar Association in partnership with the National Institute for Trial Advocacy. Mr. Mogerman is a past-chair of the Family Law Section of the Bar Association of Metropolitan St. Louis.

Mr. Mogerman is a frequent lecturer for local, statewide, and national programs,on a variety of topics related to the practice of marital and family law. He has also written articles for legal journals including the Journal of the American Academy of Matrimonial Lawyers and the St. Louis Bar Journal.

He has authored the chapters entitled "Conflicts of Law" and "Characterization and Division of Property in Divorce" in the Missouri Bar desk book, *Missouri Family Law,* now in its seventh edition.

Mr. Mogerman and his wife Dee are the parents of three adult sons.

Mr. Mogerman may be reached through his website:
www.zermanmogerman.com

Joseph J. Kodner, Esq., is a partner in the firm of Zerman Mogerman LLC. He graduated Phi Beta Kappa from the Washington University in 1999 and obtained his juris doctorate from the Washington University School of Law in 2003. Following graduation, Mr. Kodner practiced for two years in Kansas City in the field of defense litigation. Since joining Zerman Mogerman LLC in 2005, he has limited his practice to the field of matrimonial and family law, with particular emphasis on prenuptial agreements and appellate work. In addition to his trial level work, Mr. Kodner has successfully handled numerous appellate matters in the Missouri Court of Appeals.

Mr. Kodner has spoken and written on a variety of legal topics. In addition to his other publications, Mr. Kodner co-authored the update for the most recent edition of the Missouri Bar Family Law CLE chapter on "Conflicts of Law." He has been recognized on eight separate occasions as a "Super Lawyers Rising Star" by the Missouri and Kansas Super Lawyers, a publication of Law and Politics Magazine.

Mr. Kodner is licensed to practice law in both Missouri and Kansas; he is a member of several local bar associations. Mr. Kodner and his wife Holly are the parents of two daughters.

Mr. Kodner may be reached through his website:
www.zermanmogerman.com

Divorce Titles from Addicus Books

Visit our online catalog at www.AddicusBooks.com

Divorce in Alabama: The Legal Process, Your Rights, and What to Expect $21.95

Divorce in Arizona: The Legal Process, Your Rights, and What to Expect. $21.95

Divorce in California: The Legal Process, Your Rights, and What to Expect $21.95

Divorce in Connecticut: The Legal Process, Your Rights, and What to Expect $21.95

Divorce in Florida: The Legal Process, Your Rights, and What to Expect $21.95

Divorce in Georgia: Simple Answers to Your Legal Questions $21.95

Divorce in Hawaii: The Legal Process, Your Rights, and What to Expect $21.95

Divorce in Illinois: The Legal Process, Your Rights, and What to Expect $21.95

Divorce in Kansas: The Legal Process, Your Rights, and What to Expect $21.95

Divorce in Louisiana: The Legal Process, Your Rights, and What to Expect $21.95

Divorce in Maine: The Legal Process, Your Rights, and What to Expect $21.95

Divorce in Maryland: The Legal Process, Your Rights, and What to Expect $21.95

Divorce in Michigan: The Legal Process, Your Rights, and What to Expect. $21.95

Divorce in Mississippi: The Legal Process, Your Rights, and What to Expect. $21.95

A Guide to Divorce in Missouri: Simple Answers to Complex Questions $21.95

Divorce in Nebraska: The Legal Process, Your Rights, and What to Expect—2nd Edition $21.95

Divorce in Nevada: The Legal Process, Your Rights, and What to Expect. $21.95

Divorce in New Jersey: The Legal Process, Your Rights, and What to Expect $21.95

Divorce in New York: The Legal Process, Your Rights, and What to Expect $21.95

Divorce in North Carolina: Answers to Your Legal Questions. $21.95

Divorce in Oklahoma: The Legal Process, Your Rights, and What to Expect $21.95

Divorce in Tennessee: The Legal Process, Your Rights, and What to Expect $21.95

Divorce in Virginia: The Legal Process, Your Rights, and What to Expect $21.95

Divorce in Washington: The Legal Process, Your Rights, and What to Expect $21.95

Divorce in West Virginia: The Legal Process, Your Rights, and What to Expect $21.95

Divorce in Wisconsin: The Legal Process, Your Rights, and What to Expect $21.95

Daily Meditations for Healing from Divorce: Discovering the New You. $21.95

To Order Books:
Visit us online at: www.AddicusBooks.com
Call toll free: (800) 888-4741

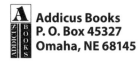

Addicus Books
P. O. Box 45327
Omaha, NE 68145

To order books from Addicus Books:

Please send:

_____copies of_____
                                             (Title of book)

        at $ _____each   TOTAL _____
        NE residents add 5% sales tax   _____

        Add Shipping/Handling
            $6.75 for first book
            $1.10 for each additional book _____

          TOTAL ENCLOSED   _____

Name _____
Address _____
City _____State_____Zip _____

      ☐ Visa   ☐ Mastercard   ☐ AMEX   ☐ Discover
Credit card number _____
Expiration date _____
Three digit CVV number on back of card _____

Order by credit card or personal check.

To Order Books:
Visit us online at: www.AddicusBooks.com
Call toll free: (800) 888-4741

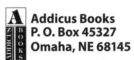

Addicus Books
P. O. Box 45327
Omaha, NE 68145